WINDOWS ON THE
WORLD OF JESUS

ALSO BY BRUCE J. MALINA
PUBLISHED BY WESTMINSTER/JOHN KNOX PRESS

Christian Origins and Cultural Anthropology:
Practical Models for Biblical Interpretation

The New Testament World (Revised Edition):
Insights from Cultural Anthropology

WINDOWS ON THE WORLD OF JESUS

Time Travel to Ancient Judea

BRUCE J. MALINA

WESTMINSTER/JOHN KNOX PRESS
Louisville, Kentucky

© 1993 Bruce J. Malina

Book Design by Publishers' WorkGroup
Cover Design by Laura Lee
Cover Photograph by Jo Bales Gallagher: Road Along the Dead Sea

First edition

This book is printed on acid-free paper that meets the American National Standards Institute Z39.48 standard. ∞

Published by Westminster/John Knox Press
Louisville, Kentucky

PRINTED IN THE UNITED STATES OF AMERICA

2 4 6 8 9 7 5 3 1

Library of Congress Cataloging-in-Publication Data

Malina, Bruce J.
    Windows on the world of Jesus : time travel to ancient Judea /
Bruce J. Malina. — 1st ed.
        p.   cm.
    Includes bibliographical references
    ISBN 0–664–25457–8 (alk. paper)

    1. Sociology, Biblical.   2. Bible.   N.T.—Criticism, interpretation, etc.
3. Palestine—Social life and customs—To 70 A.D.   4. Jews—Social life and customs—To 70 A.D.   I. Title.
BS2545.S55M35   1993
225.9'5—dc20   93–10360

CONTENTS

Preface   xi

Introduction   xiii

I. HONOR AND SHAME

Introductory Window   1

Window 1: Father and Sons   2
Meanings in Window 1: Was Jesus a Rebellious Son?   2

Window 2: Father, Son, and Daughter   5
Meanings in Window 2: Learning About Redemption   5

Window 3: Heckling a Teacher   8
Meanings in Window 3: Defending Honor in the Gospels   8

Window 4: The Avenging Cuckold   11
Meanings in Window 4: Feud Prevention   11

Window 5: Ungrateful Natives   13
Meanings in Window 5: Gratitude or Solidarity?   13

Window 6: The Violent Temple Guard   15
Meanings in Window 6: Swearing, Oath-Taking, and Honor   15

Window 7: A Teacher Without Disciples   17
Meanings in Window 7: Jesus, Abandoned Teacher?   17

Summary Window   19
For Further Reading   19

II. GENERAL INTERPERSONAL BEHAVIOR

Introductory Window   21

Window 8: Effeminate Males?   22
Meanings in Window 8: Why Jesus Is Tactile   22

Window 9: Open-hearted, Close-minded?   24
Meanings in Window 9: Why Jesus Is So Emotional   24

Window 10: Hot-tempered?   26
Meanings in Window 10: The New Testament and
    Specific Emotions   26

Window 11: Parents, Students, Teachers   29
Meanings in Window 11: Why Jesus Emphasizes Doing   29

Window 12: Performance Isn't Everything   31
Meanings in Window 12: Why Jesus Judged More than Performance   31

Window 13: Alone Means with a Group   33
Meanings in Window 13: Group Aloneness in the Gospels   33

Window 14: Age Counts More than Youth   35
Meanings in Window 14: Respect for Older Persons   35

Window 15: The "Friendly" Teacher   37
Meanings in Window 15: A World of Formality in Private and
    in Public   37

Window 16: The "Friendly" Mistress   39
Meanings in Window 16: The Social Dimensions of Christian Service   39

Window 17: A Seller's Market   42
Meanings in Window 17: Fairness Is Status-specific   42

Summary Window   45
For Further Reading   45

III. IN-GROUP

Introductory Window   47

Window 18: A Friend of a Friend   48
Meanings in Window 18: Recommendations in Early Christianity   48

Window 19: Neighbors   50
Meanings in Window 19: What Is a Neighborhood?   50

Window 20: Friendly or Nosey? 52
Meanings in Window 20: Who Is a Neighbor? 52

Window 21: Unknown Friends 55
Meanings in Window 21: Love as Group Attachment 55

Window 22: Landlords and Tenants 57
Meanings in Window 22: The Householder and Tenant Relationship 57

Window 23: Boss or Patron? 59
Meanings in Window 23: About Gifts and Favors, Divine and Human 59

Window 24: Townmates 62
Meanings in Window 24: In Israel Versus in Christ as In-Group 62

Window 25: Trust or Competence? 65
Meanings in Window 25: Jesus, In-Groups, and Core Groups 65

Window 26: Prospective Friends 67
Meanings in Window 26: Jesus and Friends of Friends 67

Window 27: Friends Feel Obligated 68
Meanings in Window 27: Christian In-Group Support 68

Summary Window 70
For Further Reading 70

IV. INTRA-FAMILY RELATIONS

Introductory Window 71

Window 28: Boys and Girls, Not Children 72
Meanings in Window 28: A Gender-divided Society 72

Window 29: Male Tasks, Female Tasks 76
Meanings in Window 29: Female Roles and Values in the Bible 76

Window 30: Parents and Children 79
Meanings in Window 30: The Parents of Sons 79

Window 31: Mothers and Sons 82
Meanings in Window 31: Mary and Jesus, Mother and Son 82

Window 32: Motherly Competition 85
Meanings in Window 32: Gospel Mothers 85

Summary Window 87
For Further Reading 87

CONTENTS

V. Out-Group

Introductory Window   89

Window 33: Polite Indifference   90
Meanings in Window 33: Why Not Jesus of Capernaum?   90

Window 34: Outsiders Don't Count   92
Meanings in Window 34: The Trial of Jesus, an Out-Group Person   92

Window 35: How to Keep Friends   93
Meanings in Window 35: Jesus' Out-Group Relationships   93

Window 36: American Spoiled Children   95
Meanings in Window 36: God's (Free) Gifts Must Be Repaid   95

Window 37: Family Dropout   97
Meanings in Window 37: Traditional Biblical Views on Friends and Enemies   97

Window 38: Rude Americans   99
Meanings in Window 38: Jesus' Public Put-downs   99

Summary Window   101
For Further Reading   101

VI. Loving-kindness

Introductory Window   103

Window 39: A Case of Bad Social Credit   104
Meanings in Window 39: Loving-Kindness Means Debt of Gratitude   104

Window 40: The Obligated, Unhappy Brother   108
Meanings in Window 40: Redeemers Pay Debts of Gratitude   108

Window 41: The Friend Who Meant Well   110
Meanings in Window 41: Ancient Service and Sales   110

Summary Window   112
For Further Reading   112

VII. Common Values

Introductory Window   113

Window 42: Never Make a Mistake   114
Meanings in Window 42: Decisions Are to Be Avoided   114

Contents

Window 43: Never Admit Ignorance   117
Meanings in Window 43: Unfamiliarity Is Not to Be Admitted   117

Window 44: Schedules Are Not Important   120
Meanings in Window 44: The Inefficiency of Others Is to Be Overlooked   120

Window 45: There Is Nothing We Don't Know   122
Meanings in Window 45: Challengers to Honor Are to Be Repulsed   122

Window 46: Honor Before Efficiency   124
Meanings in Window 46: Non-hostile Out-Group Persons Are to Be
    Encouraged   124

Window 47: Becoming Indispensable   126
Meanings in Window 47: Take Measures to Become Indispensable   126

Window 48: A Helping Hand?   130
Meanings in Window 48: Do Not Threaten the Indispensability
    of Others   130

Window 49: Becoming Indispensable: Part II   133
Meanings in Window 49: Take Measures to Become
    Indispensable: Part II   133

Window 50: Mind Your Own Opinions   135
Meanings in Window 50: Mistakes and Errors Are Rarely One's Own   135

Window 51: Know-Who Is What Counts   137
Meanings in Window 51: Responsibility Is to Be Avoided   137

Window 52: Mind Your Own Status   142
Meanings in Window 52: Superiors Are Always Right   142

Window 53: More on Making Friends   146
Meanings in Window 53: All Non–Out-Group Relations Are Personal
    Relations   146

Window 54: Small Is Beautiful, of Course   149
Meanings in Window 54: Economics and Religion Are Embedded in
    Kinship and Politics   149

Window 55: Keep It in the Family   151
Meanings in Window 55: In Everything the Family Comes First   151

Summary Window   153
For Further Reading   153

CONTENTS

VIII. CONCEPT OF TIME

Introductory Window   155

Window 56: Clock Time and Event Time   156
Meanings in Window 56: New Testament Persons Are Concerned
   About the Present   156

Window 57: Being on Time   158
Meanings in Window 57: In the New Testament, Significant Persons
   Always Come on Time   158

Window 58: Mediterranean Time Is Different   160
Meanings in Window 58: In the New Testament, Whenever Events Occur,
   They Are on Time   160

Window 59: Time Without Clocks   162
Meanings in Window 59: New Testament Persons See the Forthcoming
   Rooted in the Present   162

Window 60: Scheduling for the Present   166
Meanings in Window 60: All Plans in the New Testament Are Tentative   166

Window 61: Present Orientation   168
Meanings in Window 61: The Only Sensible Investment Is in the Present   168

Summary Window   170
For Further Reading   170

Concluding Overview   171

PREFACE

The purpose of this book is to provide a rather basic introduction to the world of the Bible, specifically to facilitate New Testament interpretation. I have prepared this book with the presupposition that all language, whether oral or written, hence including biblical language, derives its meanings from the societal system and cultural context in which the language communication originally takes place.[1] For the New Testament, this means that to read the various books in terms of the meanings of the original authors and their audiences the considerate reader will have to leap back to the time-bound and space-bound cultural context in which the authors first attempted to communicate their Good News. Theologically, this is an "incarnational" approach to the New Testament. The Word of God is considered here as fully bound up with the flesh and blood symbolic world of meaning of the first-century Eastern Mediterranean.

What follows is a series of Windows that look into the world of Jesus and his contemporaries. A thoughtful look through these Windows is intended to offer rather quick and easy access to that first-century Mediterranean world. These Windows are then related to actual segments of the New Testament, and at times to passages from writings from the same cultural area and closely related to New Testament times. By using the scenarios observed through these Windows to gain facility in interacting within a foreign world of meaning, I hope that readers will assimilate some of the fundamental perspectives of the culture of the ancient Mediterranean. These perspectives are some of the fundamental viewpoints shared by New Testament persons.

The approach followed in this book is based on the work of a team of researchers who, nearly a generation ago, provided theoretical and practical guides to help persons assimilate alien cultures.[2] And it goes without saying that the world of the New Testament is an alien world for contemporary North Americans. I would hope that this sort of introduction to the first-century Mediterranean might have as much value for contemporary New Testament readers, professional and nonprofessional, as other sorts of introductions to the New Testament.

NOTES

1. See my essay on how reading works: "Reading Theory Perspective," in Jerome H. Neyrey, ed., *The Social World of Luke-Acts: Models for Interpretation* (Peabody, Mass.: Hendrickson, 1991), 3–23. It may be important to note that a lack of sense of history was equally a feature of the first-century Mediterranean. People believed things were always the way they presently were. This is why they believed that history offered valuable lessons, for the past indicated and exemplified unchanging features of human behavior, since human beings and their societies never change. First-century members of the house of Israel read the Old Testament ahistorically. Consequently the Old Testament provided ready and direct input into their contemporary social life.

2. For more information see Terrence R. Mitchell, Jerome Gagerman, and Samuel Schwartz, *Greek Culture Assimilator*, Group Effectiveness Research Laboratory (Urbana, Ill.: University of Illinois Press, 1969). The proven value of learning another culture by means of such a process has been well documented; see Martin M. Chemers, Fred E. Fiedler, Duangduen Lekhyananda, and Lawrence M. Stolurow, "Some Effects of Cultural Training on Leadership in Heterocultural Task Groups," *International Journal of Psychology* 1 (1966): 301–314. And more recntly, see Richard W. Brislin, Kenneth Cushner, Craig Cherrie, and Mahealani Yong, *Intercultural Interactions: A Practical Guide* (Cross-cultural Research and Methodology Series 9; Beverly Hills, Calif.: Sage, 1986).

INTRODUCTION

This book is intended as a basic introduction to the New Testament. It introduces the reader to the New Testament by means of a compact self-help course in Mediterranean cultural anthropology. Most readers will initially find this point of view a bit odd. The pay-off will come when the reader returns to reading the New Testament texts. For the purpose of this approach is to enable the reader to acquire some insight into the social system prevailing in the first-century social contexts shared by Jesus, Paul, and the other persons who people the pages of the New Testament. If the meanings that people share derive from their social systems, it is of little value to study the Greek of the New Testament or the Hebrew of the Old if one simply maintains a North American appreciation of how the world works. In fact many U.S. students learn to speak U.S. English in a number of foreign languages by avoiding the social system of the people who are native speakers of those foreign languages. This is especially the case for students devoted to self-study.

The compact course presented in this book proceeds in terms of Windows through which the reader gets to view scenes or scenarios of people interacting with each other. The question at the close of each scenario is presented with the purpose of helping the reader to assimilate various basic dimensions of the first-century Mediterranean view of life. This approach provides an alternative to the more conventional methods of reading books and essays about the late Israelite social history, watching films and slides on first-century Judea and Galilee, and the like. While these conventional methods may be of real value, they fall far short of their potential unless the student is provided with some understanding of the values and meanings shared by the people of the time.

The set of scenarios presented here has been selected on the basis of general, well-known methods used to increase a person's skill at interacting with people from a different culture. After all, any Bible reader is necessarily a foreigner in an extremely alien culture, for the social world of Jesus and Paul is removed from us in time, space, social structures, and culture. In terms of time, consider those tremendous events that block out our vision of the first-century Mediterranean, such as the Industrial Revolution, the American Revolution, the Enlightenment, the Renaissance, the Reformation, and the like. These most significant shapers of our modern experience intervene between the modern Bible reader and the times of the biblical authors much like a set of two-thousand-year-thick lenses. With such lenses firmly in place before our eyes, it becomes quite difficult to consider the past on its own terms. Our accumulated human history always seems to get in the way.

Moreover, in terms of social system, there is little to link modern Americans with the values, institutions, and concerns of the Mediterranean world of today. And what about the values, institutions, and concerns of ancient Mediterranean peoples?

This sort of introductory book should make the modern Bible reader a more considerate reader. In order to help bridge the gap of time and culture, the book presents a series of episodes formulated from first-century Israelite and Mediterranean data. These episodes are intended to illuminate important aspects of the culture of New Testament times, the target culture of this book. These aspects are known to have existed in the first-century Mediterranean and are frequently evidenced in New Testament writings. They include the values called "honor" and "shame," relationships among family members, among groups, the concept of time, and the like.

Now for the layout of this book. From the Table of Contents, the reader will see that the book presents a series of Windows under various headings or perspectives. Each Window looks out upon episodes of persons interacting. These episodes are purposely anachronistic, for they feature twentieth-century Americans interacting with first-century Mediterraneans, at times in ancient settings, at other times in modern settings. This state of affairs is not unlike that mirrored in the scenarios that the twentieth-century Bible reader brings to the first-century New Testament.

Each series of Windows has an introductory Window briefly describing the value or perspective at issue. However, at the end of each single scenario or Window there is a question that calls for an explanation of the episode in terms of the alien social system.

The author's answer to each question follows the Window. This answer consists of the range of meanings carried by the interaction described in the Window, followed by a number of biblical passages in which the value or perspective at issue is evidenced. The successful use of this book depends on the reader's thinking through the question and providing an answer or a range of answers to the initial questions before moving on to read the suggested answer and biblical passages. The cultural differences between contemporary North American ways of living and perceiving and first-century Mediterranean ways should grow increasingly apparent. In the process of responding to these questions, the Bible reader should readily perceive and assimilate some of the basic cultural cues of the ancient Mediterranean.

Since this book presents an anthropological approach to reading the New Testament, a distinctive and surprising feature for some readers will be the absence of the word "Jew" or the adjective "Jewish." The New Testament Greek word *Ioudaios* is always translated "Judean." There are two reasons for this. The first reason is that people and animate beings in the ancient Mediterranean were labeled in terms of their geographic place of origin. And the place of origin labeled by the Greek *Ioudaios* was Judea. Thus, Romans were Romans because they came from Rome. Judeans were Judeans because they came from Judea.

In in-group context, however, Judeans labeled themselves as the house of Israel. This house of Israel included Judeans, Galileans, Pereans, and those who had their origin in the land of Israel, but emigrated. While the house of Israel divided itself geographically into these smaller units, to outsiders everyone of the house of Israel was called a Judean. And the behavior typical of these Judeans was called Judaism. This is just like the situation for the various Hellenic peoples, lumped together as Hellenes (Greeks), with their typical behavior called Hellenism.

A second reason for translating *Ioudaios* as "Judean" and not "Jew" is that words take their meaning from social systems. In our U.S. experience, many of us know Jews and know about Jews. Now as a number of contemporary American scholars have demonstrated (for example, Jacob Neusner, Shaye Cohen), the religion of contemporary Jews is rooted in the formation of the Babylonian Talmud of the sixth century A.D. What emerged was "normative Judaism," the Pharisaic scribalism that is the matrix of today's Jewish religious belief and practice.

In other words, today there are in fact Christians and Jews. But there really were none in the first century. In Palestine Israelite Yahwism comprised various currents: Pharisaic, Christian (Messianic), Herodian, Sadducean, Essene, and the like. The chief opponents of the Galilean Jesus of Nazareth were the Judeans, that is, fellow Israelites from Judea. To Pilate, a Roman foreigner, Jesus was sarcastically "King of the Judeans."

If this is all a bit confusing, it is either because Bible translators have not perceived the question of the meaning of words or because they have chosen not to abandon traditional terminology. In this work, I shall try to be culturally sensitive to the ancients; hence I shall avoid the terms "Jew" and "Jewish."

At the close of each set of Windows, the reader will find a summary of the features presented in them. After that the author has provided a list of suggested readings to help satisfy curiosity and deepen the initial insights provided by this book. The book concludes with a list of all the scenarios and indexes.

I

HONOR AND SHAME

INTRODUCTORY WINDOW

The organizing principle of Mediterranean society has been and continues to be belongingness, structured primarily by means of the family. In other words, for a Mediterranean, success in life means maintaining ties to other persons within sets of significant groups. The central group in this set is one's kinship group. A person's identity depends on belonging to and being accepted by the family. However, such belonging and acceptance depend on a person's adhering to the traditional rules of order by which Mediterranean families are organized and maintained. And those traditional rules of order are rooted in the complementary codes of honor and shame.

Honor refers to a person's (or group's) claim to worth, along with the acknowledgment of that worth by others in the community. Honor is socially acknowledged worth. In the Mediterranean world of the past and present, honor is a core value. Since it is a value, honor is also a quality that inheres in one's behavior.

Honorable persons manifest the quality of honor in what they say and do. Persons who show concern for their honor are said to have (positive) shame. On the other hand, persons can lose their honor, especially through interactions with others. When in the estimation of the community, a person is judged to have been bested by another, that person is said to be shamed. A good honor rating is crucially necessary for a meaningful human social existence, much as a good credit rating is in our society.

In the Windows that follow, Americans of various sorts are involved in interactions with Mediterranean Judeans, either as witnesses or as participants. A careful consideration of these Windows along with thoughtful regard to the questions that follow each of them will provide increased insight into the values of honor and shame.

Father and Sons

Hoe Didor, Hank Wilkin's neighbor, was extremely infuriated one morning. Hank went up to Hoe and asked him what was bothering him.

"Yesterday," Hoe said, "I went out to the village to find my sons and ask them to help me finish some work that remained in the field. I ran into them in the busy village square and asked them to come and help me finish the work. They told me they were busy at the moment putting a roof on a neighbor's house but that they would come to help tomorrow or the day after." The response sounded reasonable, so Hank could not figure out what made Hoe so inordinately angry.

Why was Hoe so infuriated?

MEANINGS IN WINDOW 1

Was Jesus a Rebellious Son?

Hoe was angry because his sons dishonored him in public. Because the focal social institution in the Mediterranean is kinship, the role of a father means status on the social ladder. When a father commands his children to do something, and they obey him, they treat him honorably. Other people seeing this acknowledge that he is an honorable father. But should a father command his children and they procrastinate or disobey, they dishonor him. The father's peers would feel free to ridicule him, thereby acknowledging his lack of honor as a father.

At times non-Mediterraneans insist that honor is not a central value because it differs from community to community. However, it is important to note from the beginning that honor is not a type of action or a type of social role. Rather honor is a value. And what differs is the way in which various communities evaluate actions and roles. In other words, various groups of people might evaluate quite different behaviors as honorable. Think of what a group of thieves might hold to be of worth, or what a group of merchants might think honorable. Yet all Mediterraneans make a claim to honor.

Moreover, U.S. persons must realize that it is highly doubtful that a Mediterranean would get angry over unforeseen economic outlays. In this first Window, one might say Didor got angry because perhaps it might rain and his fieldwork required dry weather, so his sons should have come immediately. The fact is that even if the neglect of the fieldwork did lead to loss of money, that would not lead to anger. Money is valued because it begets honor, and money that cannot be converted to honor is not very socially useful.

Israelite tradition had some harsh lessons for the son who shamed his father (or mother). The legislation in Deuteronomy directs:

> If a man has a stubborn and rebellious son, who will not obey the voice of his father or the voice of his mother, and, though they chastise him, will not give heed to them, then his father and his mother shall take hold of him and bring him out to the elders of his city at the gate of the place where he lives, and they shall say to the elders of his city, "This our son is stubborn and rebellious, he will not obey our voice; he is a glutton and a drunkard." Then all the men of the city shall stone him to death with stones; so you shall purge the evil from your midst; and all Israel shall hear, and fear (Deut. 21:18–21).

The point is that a consistently disobedient son is like a glutton and drunkard. Both of the last-named categories are socially obnoxious. They deprive the family of its honor rating since they are negative qualities. And all qualities revealed in children, whether positive or negative, are proverbially ascribed to their parents. For honor derives from the fact of birth ("Like mother, like daughter," Ezek. 16:44; like father, like son, Matt. 11:27; see also Deut. 23:2; 2 Kings 9:22; Isa. 57:3; Hos. 1:2; Sirach 23:25–26; 30:7). Being born into an honorable family makes one honorable since the family is the repository of the honor of illustrious ancestors and their accumulated acquired honor. One of the major purposes of genealogies in the Bible is to set out a person's honor lines. Genealogies situate a person on a traditional ladder of statuses. Genealogies underscore a person's ascribed honor (thus Matt. 1:2–16; Luke 3:23–38; questions about Jesus' family and origin look to the same thing in Mark 6:3; Matt. 13:54–57; Luke 4:22; John 7:40–42; for Paul read Rom. 11:1; Phil. 3:5).

Thus a consistently disobedient son, like a wayward daughter, casts grave doubts on a family's claim to honor. Such persons dishonor their parents by not obeying a command or request given in public.

The behavior of Absalom with regard to his father, David, should be read in the light of this Window (read 2 Samuel 13–18).

Of course when Jesus announces that his true brothers, sisters, and mother are those who do the will of God, he surely places his honor and that of his family in question (Mark 3:31–35; Matt. 12:46–50; Luke 8:19–21). Furthermore, the Gospel tradition tells us he ate at times with "tax collectors and sinners" (Mark 2:15–16; Matt. 9:10–11; Luke 5:30; 15:1), and along with this notice, he was accused of being a "glutton and drunkard" to boot (Matt. 11:19; Luke 7:34). This obviously is just the opposite of the behavior of an obedient son who brings honor to his family! Would not the injunction of Deuteronomy 21:18–21 cited above apply to Jesus as a disobedient and rebellious son? What might excuse Jesus' shameful behavior?

In terms of the code of honor and shame, only if Jesus were of higher, socially unassailable status could this sort of behavior be countenanced, even praised. For higher-status people are superior to the obligations of ordinary persons who simply cannot understand what higher-status people are up to. The informed reader of the Gospel narrative is clued into the probabilities of such a status by the voice from the sky at Jesus' baptism, where readers are told that God is "well pleased" with Jesus (Mark 1:11; Matt. 3:17; Luke 3:22), and again at Jesus' Transformation, where readers are told to "listen to him" (Mark 9:7; Matt. 17:5; Luke 9:35).

Father, Son, and Daughter

Steve Crown's business in first-century Judea took him through a number of villages outside of Jerusalem. One day as he passed through a certain village, he saw a group of old men congratulating one of their peers. His curiosity excited, Steve asked a bystander what was the occasion for the celebration. The bystander said that the old man's cronies were congratulating him because his oldest son, who just returned from a village on the Mount of Olives, had killed the old man's daughter, who had eloped with her boyfriend. Steve was rather horrified at the thought.

Why was this homicide an occasion for congratulations?

MEANINGS IN WINDOW 2

Learning About Redemption

Marriages in the first-century Mediterranean were generally arranged by parents. By eloping, the daughter seriously dishonored her father and her family. It was the oldest son's duty to restore the honor of the father. In this case the son restored family honor by killing the offending member of the family. Such behavior on the part of the daughter of an honorable father casts grave doubt on the father's honor. The father as father has the right and duty to decide on the marriage of his daughter; she is embedded in his family. That is to say, she is not an individual, free to make up her own mind. Rather, she is considered as always bound, tied, connected with the father and his family. Her main concern is to act in a way that mirrors the values, concerns, and honor of her father and his family. What she personally thinks and feels is of no significance, and is best kept to herself. The daughter must acknowledge her father's status relative to her since this is his God-given rank on the status ladder. By eloping, the daughter shows a total disregard for her father's power over her. She dismisses and disregards his authority, his social control. The community will be quick to deny, in word and deed, the father's claim to social standing, hence his honor. Of course his daughter dishonored him, and the community would deny his claim to honor since he could not even control his daughter as fathers should.

On the other hand, by doing away with the dishonoring family member, the oldest son restored the family's standing. The old men were congratulating their peer on the fact that he raised a solid and upstanding son, a son who is concerned about his father's honor and that of his family.

Throughout the Bible, concern with "redemption" is always about restoring and maintaining the honor of a family. Acts of redemption are rooted in a society concerned with honor, with the restoration of lost honor and the maintenance of regained honor. At times redemption involves ransoming the life of another by exchange or purchase; at times it involves freeing another by force. Whatever the mode, the sought-for outcome is always the restoration of lost honor symbolized by persons or possessions displaced from the family.

While redemption takes on many dimensions, the family member who restores the honor of the family head or of the family in general is called a "redeemer" (Hebrew, *go'el*). The redeemer as a family member responsible for maintenance of family honor is known in Joshua (20:3, 5, 9) and especially in Ruth (2:20; 3:13; 4:1–15). He is a blood avenger, responsible for vendettas in feuding contexts (Num. 35:12, 19, 21, 24–28; Deut. 19:6, 12; Josh. 20:3, 5, 9; 2 Sam. 14:11). He is also responsible for getting family members out of slavery (Lev. 25:48) or for recovering family possessions (Lev. 25:25, 48ff.).

From the book of Ruth we learn that the redeemer has the obligation to buy back the lands of a deceased relative to keep the possessions in the family. He likewise is expected to marry his childless relative's widow, to have children in the latter's name. Finally in Ruth, we see how the redeemer can transfer his right and duty to another close relative (read Ruth 2:20; 3:9; and 4:1–12).

This role is a favorite image of God in the theology of Second Isaiah. Consider the following:

> Fear not, you worm Jacob,
>   you men of Israel!
> I will help you, says the LORD;
>   your Redeemer is the Holy One of Israel (Isa. 41:14).

> Thus says the LORD,
>   your Redeemer, the Holy One of Israel:
> "For your sake I will send to Babylon
>   and break down all the bars,
>   and the shouting of the Chaldeans
>   will be turned to lamentations" (Isa. 43:14).

> Thus says the LORD, the King of Israel
>   and his Redeemer, the LORD of hosts:
> "I am the first and I am the last;
>   besides me there is no god" (Isa. 44:6).

> Thus says the LORD, your Redeemer,
>   who formed you from the womb:
> "I am the LORD, who made all things,
>   who stretched out the heavens alone,
>   who spread out the earth—Who was with me?" (Isa. 44:24).

Our Redeemer—the LORD of hosts is his name—
  is the Holy One of Israel (Isa. 47:4).

Thus says the LORD,
  your Redeemer, the Holy One of Israel:
"I am the LORD your God,
  who teaches you to profit,
  who leads you in the way you should go" (Isa. 48:17).

Thus says the LORD,
  the Redeemer of Israel and his Holy One,
to one deeply despised, abhorred by the nations,
  the servant of rulers:
"Kings shall see and arise;
  princes, and they shall prostrate themselves;
because of the LORD, who is faithful,
  the Holy One of Israel, who has chosen you" (Isa. 49:7).

I will make your oppressors eat their own flesh,
  and they shall be drunk with their own blood as with wine.
Then all flesh shall know
  that I am the LORD your Savior,
  and your Redeemer, the Mighty One of Jacob (Isa. 49:26).

For your Maker is your husband,
  the LORD of hosts is his name;
and the Holy One of Israel is your Redeemer,
  the God of the whole earth he is called (Isa. 54:5).

In overflowing wrath for a moment
  I hid my face from you,
but with everlasting love I will have compassion on you,
  says the LORD, your Redeemer (Isa. 54:8).

You shall suck the milk of nations,
  you shall suck the breast of kings;
and you shall know that I, the LORD, am your Savior
  and your Redeemer, the Mighty One of Jacob (Isa. 60:16).

According to these passages from Second Isaiah, what are the attributes or features of the behavior of a redeemer? What is God like as redeemer?

In the New Testament, the God of Israel is the source of redemption, as in the hymn "Blessed be the Lord God of Israel, for he has visited and redeemed his people" (Luke 1:68). Yet as the disciples state at the end of that Gospel concerning Jesus, "But we had hoped that he was the one to redeem Israel" (Luke 24:21). Of course, if Jesus is redeemer, it means he acted like the brother who restores a family's lost honor, "who gave himself for us to redeem us from all iniquity and to purify for himself a people of his own who are zealous for good deeds" (Titus 2:14; see Rom. 3:24; 1 Cor. 1:30; Eph. 1:7; 4:30).

7

Heckling a Teacher

As Henry Naparla and his wife did their shopping in Jerusalem, they could hear a teacher on one of the street corners, instructing his following about greed in the marketplace. Upon inquiry, they learned that the teacher was a well-known expert in ethical matters with a rather large following in various towns. Soon another small group, elegantly dressed, approached. One of that group asked the teacher a seemingly innocent question about how the teacher and his group obtain their support since they do not seem to work for it. The teacher retorted with the question: "So how do lazy rich people like you gain their support?" Henry and his wife laughed. But they were surprised that an honored teacher would have recourse to such an ostensibly improper reply.

Why did the teacher answer the way he did?

MEANINGS IN WINDOW 3

Defending Honor in the Gospels

The teacher perceived the question of the well-dressed group's spokesman as a challenge to his honor. In order to maintain his own honor and that of his following, the teacher had to respond to the challenge with a put-down.

First-century Mediterraneans, for the most part, live their lives in public. Honor comes from public acknowledgment of worth. An attack on honor, as in this scene, requires a forceful defense, a response that might put the attackers on the defensive. Such a successful defense of honor in the social "game" of challenge and response results in renewed grants of honor. Such grants of honor grow to varying degrees of fame and glory.

Answering a question with a question is typical of challenge-response interactions. And when such interactions are in play, rarely does the point of discussion stay in fixed focus. Rather the point of the interaction is challenge-response, honor and shame, and this is always in firmly fixed attention, whether consciously or latently.

To appreciate this public defense of honor and the put-down of opponents, consider the following responses of Jesus to various challengers. Note how a question is repulsed with an often insulting counterquestion:

> Now John's disciples and the Pharisees were fasting; and people came and said to him, "Why do John's disciples and the disciples of the Pharisees fast, but your disciples do not fast?" And Jesus said to them, "Can the wedding guests fast while the bridegroom is with them?" (Mark 2:18–19).

8

And the Pharisees said to him, "Look, why are they doing what is not lawful on the sabbath?" And he said to them, "Have you never read what David did, when he was in need and was hungry, he and those who were with him: how he entered the house of God, when Abiathar was high priest, and ate the bread of the Presence, which it is not lawful for any but the priests to eat, and also gave it to those who were with him?" (Mark 2:24–26).

And the Pharisees and the scribes asked him, "Why do your disciples not live according to the tradition of the elders, but eat with hands defiled?" And he said to them, "Well did Isaiah prophesy of you hypocrites, as it is written,
'This people honors me with their lips,
but their heart is far from me;
in vain do they worship me,
teaching as doctrines the precepts of men.'
You leave the commandment of God, and hold fast the tradition of men."
And he said to them, "You have a fine way of rejecting the commandment of God, in order to keep your tradition! For Moses said, 'Honor your father and your mother'; and, 'He who speaks evil of father or mother, let him surely die'; but you say, 'If a man tells his father or his mother, What you would have gained from me is Corban' (that is, given to God)—then you no longer permit him to do anything for his father or mother, thus making void the word of God through your tradition which you hand on. And many such things you do" (Mark 7:5–13).

And when he had entered the house, and left the people, his disciples asked him about the parable. And he said to them, "Then are you also without understanding? Do you not see that whatever goes into a man from outside cannot defile him, since it enters, not his heart but his stomach, and so passes on?" (Thus he declared all foods clean.) And he said, "What comes out of a man is what defiles a man. For from within, out of the heart of man, come evil thoughts, fornication, theft, murder, adultery, coveting, wickedness, deceit, licentiousness, envy, slander, pride, foolishness. All these evil things come from within, and they defile a man" (Mark 7:17–23).

And Pharisees came up and in order to test him asked, "Is it lawful for a man to divorce his wife?" He answered them, "What did Moses command you?" (Mark 10:2–3).

And as he was setting out on his journey, a man ran up and knelt before him, and asked him, "Good Teacher, what must I do to inherit eternal life?" And Jesus said to him, "Why do you call me good? No one is good but God alone" (Mark 10:17–18).

And they came again to Jerusalem. And as he was walking in the temple, the chief priests and the scribes and the elders came to him, and they said to him, "By what authority are you doing these things, or who gave you this authority to do them?" Jesus said to them, "I will ask you a question; answer me, and I will tell you by what authority I do these things. Was the baptism of John from heaven or from men? Answer me." And they argued with one another, "If we say, 'From heaven,' he will say, 'Why then did you not believe him?' But shall we say, 'From men'?"—they were afraid of the people, for all held that John was a real prophet.

So they answered Jesus, "We do not know." And Jesus said to them, "Neither will I tell you by what authority I do these things" (Mark 11:27–33).

And they sent to him some of the Pharisees and some of the Herodians, to entrap him in his talk. And they came and said to him, "Teacher, we know that you are true, and care for no man; for you do not regard the position of men, but truly teach the way of God. Is it lawful to pay taxes to Caesar, or not? Should we pay them, or should we not?" But knowing their hypocrisy, he said to them, "Why put me to the test? Bring me a coin, and let me look at it." And they brought one. And he said to them, "Whose likeness and inscription is this?" They said to him, "Caesar's." Jesus said to them, "Render to Caesar the things that are Caesar's, and to God the things that are God's." And they were amazed at him (Mark 12:13–17).

And Sadducees came to him, who say that there is no resurrection; and they asked him a question, saying, "Teacher, Moses wrote for us that if a man's brother dies and leaves a wife, but leaves no child, the man must take the wife, and raise up children for his brother. There were seven brothers; the first took a wife, and when he died left no children; and the second took her, and died, leaving no children; and the third likewise; and the seven left no children. Last of all the woman also died. In the resurrection whose wife will she be? For the seven had her as wife." Jesus said to them, "Is not this why you are wrong, that you know neither the scriptures nor the power of God? For when they rise from the dead, they neither marry nor are given in marriage, but are like angels in heaven. And as for the dead being raised, have you not read in the book of Moses, in the passage about the bush, how God said to him, 'I am the God of Abraham, and the God of Isaac, and the God of Jacob'? He is not God of the dead, but of the living; you are quite wrong" (Mark 12:18–27).

The Avenging Cuckold

Over the weekend, the English-language Jerusalem paper carried a story about how a man killed another whom he had, in fact, expected to discover with his wife in the bedroom of their house. For it seems that Moe Tissa heard from others that his wife and Shamir the Troll were having an affair. Moe knew of their assignation that day. So with full premeditation, he got a sword and killed Shamir the Troll.

All the people in the neighborhood agreed that Moe behaved quite properly by killing the adulterer. Yet the American community in the city felt such premeditated murder should not go unpunished.

Why did the local people think it was just for Moe to kill the adulterer?

MEANINGS IN WINDOW 4

Feud Prevention

Only by killing the adulterer could the husband maintain his honor. Adultery by definition means challenging the honor of another male through the females embedded in his honor. Wives and unmarried daughters (and guests) are seen to belong within the social space of the husband and father. To act with impunity toward those embedded in his social space is to challenge his honor. The challenged male must defend his honor by eliminating the challenger from that space—and in matters of adultery, the usual way to eliminate the challenger from that space is to totally eliminate the challenger.

Since adultery always means dishonoring a male by having sexual relations with his wife, adultery in the ancient Mediterranean is never something a husband can inflict upon his wife. Women can commit adultery, but adultery cannot be committed against women. Such thinking is based on the view that women are embedded in males, that males symbolize honor and have as their task defending the family against dishonor.

Adultery is a serious challenge to male honor and the family's honor as well. The seriousness of a challenge would depend on whether the challenge to honor is revocable or not, whether the social boundaries can be readily repaired or not, whether the implied or actual deprivation of honor is light, significant, or extreme and total. Thus challenges or transgressions of a person's boundaries run into increasing degrees of seriousness. The most significant degree of seriousness involves extreme and total dishonor of another with no revocation possible. This is outrage and would include murder, adultery, kidnapping, total

11

social degradation of a male (or one of his family members) by depriving him of all he needs for his status, in sum, all the things listed in the second half of the Ten Commandments. These in fact are the items listed there: outrages against one's fellow male Israelites that are simply not revocable but require vengeance. These behaviors are explicitly prohibited in the Ten Commandments in order to head off feuding and the endless vengeance provoked by "getting even" or "getting satisfaction." The prohibitions have as their purpose to maintain internal harmony in the house of Israel. They thus look to in-group stability (see Windows 18–27).

Consider the story of David, Uriah, and Bathsheba. The high-statused David does as he pleases with his subjects. Rather than fearing revenge by Bathsheba's loyal husband or anyone else, David, because of his high status, can have the man killed "honorably" and with impunity. Only equals can play the honor game of challenge and response. Yet Nathan the prophet informs David that his behavior is shameful and insulting to God. Even though he eliminated the threat of "satisfaction" by Bathsheba's husband, yet God will avenge his shameful deeds nonetheless with the death of his offspring and the curse of a permanent "sword" within his house (read 2 Samuel 11–12). Again, adultery (and murder) against in-group members, behaviors intimately bound up with revenge and feuding, are unbefitting the king of Israel, whom God must chastise to maintain societal harmony with proper exemplary behavior.

Ungrateful Natives

One day a group of Americans living in Judea were commenting to each other how when they thanked their Judean friends for anything, the "Thank you" repeatedly set frowns on their friends' faces. A Judean once mentioned how it is so typical of Americans to say "Thank you" for this and "Thank you" for that—and how irritating it was. Friends do not bother with such frequent and incessant "Thank you's." Americans should learn to stop behaving that way.

Why did the American habit of frequently expressing gratitude with a "Thank you" so irritate the Judeans?

Gratitude or Solidarity?

Judeans refrain from saying "Thank you" because the phrase is actually used to mean "No more, thank you," or "Enough, thank you." To say "Thank you" to a person who is a social equal, more or less, means "No more, thank you," in the sense that "I do not intend to interact with you anymore!" So to thank someone for his or her help means "I will not be needing you anymore in the future." It means an end to an ongoing in-group relationship, an end to the possibility of a growing friendship. This is what irritates the Judeans and other Mediterraneans, even though they sense this is not what Americans mean. It is not that Judeans take gratitude for granted. We shall see that in-group obligations involve a continuous repayment of one's debts of gratitude (see Windows 39–41). Further, since they rarely say "Thank you" in their interactions, it is equally untrue to think that ancient Judeans (or modern Mediterraneans) are simply an ungrateful people, or that they presume the world owes them a living anyway. While this attitude may be true of contemporary Israelis, it is not true of first-century Judeans.

On the other hand, for a Judean to thank a high-ranking social superior (such as the king, some Roman prefect, or God) is to acknowledge a favor received, undeserved as it was. One cannot deserve anything from such high-ranking patrons, nor can they become members of one's in-group. They are simply too remote in a social sense. But public acknowledgement is expected. Such acknowledgment redounds to the honor and glory of the high-ranking social superior.

There is a famous passage in Luke that is quite mysterious to modern Bible readers, a passage that can be explained in terms of the information provided in this Window:

And as he entered a village, he was met by ten lepers, who stood at a distance and lifted up their voices and said, "Jesus, Master, have mercy on us." When he saw them he said to them, "Go and show yourselves to the priests." And as they went they were cleansed. Then one of them, when he saw that he was healed, turned back, praising God with a loud voice; and he fell on his face at Jesus' feet, giving him thanks. Now he was a Samaritan. Then said Jesus, "Were not ten cleansed? Where are the nine? Was no one found to return and give praise to God except this foreigner?" And he said to him, "Rise and go your way; your faith has made you well" (Luke 17:12–19).

Given Mediterranean attitudes toward gratitude, one might empathize with the nine who did not come to say "Thank you," since they might require Jesus and his healing power once more in the future. Why thank him and break off the interaction? Furthermore, the nature of first-century Mediterranean "leprosy" was quite different from what we call leprosy today (Hansen's disease). Leprosy then was more of a recurrent skin eruption in various forms, like mold on the walls of a cold damp house or on wool (read Lev. 13:1–14:57). Furthermore, in the passage cited from Luke, the fact that the nine did not express gratitude might likewise indicate that Jesus was not considered a high-ranking social superior by those who were healed from the house of Israel.

On the other hand, the Samaritan's "Thank you" indicates that this person saw no more need for recourse to Jesus. His healing was once-for-all. This perspective fits Luke's understanding of Jesus and his ministry as a new Jubilee in which God would refashion everything, making the sick whole once-for-all (read the public inaugural of Jesus in the Nazareth synagogue in Luke 4:16–21: the Jubilee is alluded to in the phrase: "to proclaim the acceptable year of the Lord").

The Violent Temple Guard

While pushing his way through Jerusalem's market, Wally Wagner heard a merchant guarantee the quality of his goods by saying: "I swear it, by Jerusalem, that this cloth is of the best quality." A temple guard was walking by when the merchant made his oath. The guard immediately struck the merchant over the head with a stick. Harsh words between the men followed. Wally was quite taken aback by this sudden outburst of violence.

Why did the guard hit the merchant?

Swearing, Oath-Taking, and Honor

The temple guard believed the merchant was calling God to witness to the quality of his goods, thus demeaning God's honor. Those born and raised in a society where honor is paramount know it is their obligation to defend the honor of persons who are extremely prominent on the same social ranking that includes them as well. For a member of the house of Israel, such prominent persons include God, the king and his family, the high priest and his family, local aristocrats who serve as patrons, and the like. Such persons are considered too lofty, socially speaking, to be challenged and besmirched by ordinary people. They do not stoop to defend their honor—unless it is totally disregarded by all in the population. In ordinary circumstances, however, it is up to upright citizens to defend the honor of their social superiors, and God is the most lofty of all social superiors.

To defend God's honor against offenses in words (blasphemy) is to gain honor for oneself as well, since other upstanding members of society will second such a defense and thus heap honor upon the defender of God's honor.

The Mediterranean is an in-group–out-group world (see Windows 18–38). Persons in such social settings feel perfectly free to lie to and deceive out-group members with impunity. This is quite honorable. Now what of situations where some truthfulness is expected, as in buying and selling? This is where swearing or nonlegal oath-making comes into play. The purpose of such swearing (for example, in business: "I swear to God this is a healthy jackass") is to eliminate ambiguity and make explicit one's true intentions. An oath activates a type of implicit curse (e.g., if the jackass is sick and dies, God will punish me for calling God to witness to an untruth, hence for dishonoring God). And public opinion judges a person dishonored if he or she does not submit to an

15

oath. (Read the law regarding a wife suspected of adultery in Num. 5:11–31; see also Luke 1:73; Acts 2:30; 23:12, 14–21; Heb. 7:20–28.) In one of the antitheses of the Sermon on the Mount, we have Jesus' critique of such oath-making in business:

> Again you have heard that it was said to the men of old, "You shall not swear falsely, but shall perform to the Lord what you have sworn." But I say to you, Do not swear at all, either by heaven, for it is the throne of God, or by the earth, for it is his footstool, or by Jerusalem, for it is the city of the great King. And do not swear by your head, for you cannot make one hair white or black. Let what you say be simply "Yes" or "No"; anything more than this comes from evil (Matt. 5:33–37).

The moral teaching here is about truth in advertising, especially when God is required to be co-sponsor. If one makes an oath to another, then only the oath-maker, not the other person, can be dishonored after the oath. By putting God to witness, the oath-maker dishonors God, should he or she be lying or deceiving.

Like the temple guard in the scenario who comes forward to defend God's honor, Jesus does the same in this saying in Matthew but without using physical force.

A Teacher Without Disciples

Stu Gabbler and a couple of his Judean friends were talking about the political situation in Judea when they decided to step into a shop for a glass of wine. As they entered the shop, they could hear the din of a small crowd that gathered outside behind them. The crowd stood about a Torah-teacher who complained bitterly about the Jerusalem Temple personnel, taxes to Rome, and the elite's lack of concern for ordinary people. After a while, various dissenting voices in the small crowd grew louder. Soon the crowd broke up, leaving the would-be teacher standing all alone. In the wine shop, all the customers began to laugh at the teacher. They even made insulting gestures in his direction. Stu could not figure out what was so funny.

What was the reason for the mocking laughter?

Jesus, Abandoned Teacher?

People observing the incident laughed because a teacher whose following abandons him proves he is not worthy of the honor of a teacher's status. Indeed he is no teacher at all. All teachers in the first century were male. The role of teacher likewise presupposed social standing in the community of males. A teacher sets forth his teaching with the expectation that at least some close disciples will agree with him. Disagreement means people do not acknowledge his teaching influence. To bystanders, if all persons standing around the teacher walk away in the course of a teaching episode, this is interpreted as a dishonor since obviously even his would-be disciples do not trust him. On the other hand, should at least his disciples believe him, see the truth of his teaching, accept what he says on his authority, then the bystanders will acknowledge that he is in fact a teacher, hence worthy of honor.

Only John recalls the tradition of Jesus' disciples walking away from him. The poignant incident occurred in the Capernaum synagogue after Jesus calls himself the Bread of Life.

> Many of his disciples, when they heard it, said, "This is a hard saying; who can listen to it?" But Jesus, knowing in himself that his disciples murmured at it, said to them, "Do you take offense at this? Then what if you were to see the Son of man ascending where he was before? It is the spirit that gives life, the flesh is of no avail; the words that I have spoken to you are spirit and life. But there are some of you that do not believe." For Jesus knew from the first who those were that did not believe, and who it was that would betray him. And he said, "This is why I told you that no one can come to me unless it is granted him by the Father."

After this many of his disciples drew back and no longer went about with him. Jesus said to the twelve, "Do you also wish to go away?" Simon Peter answered him, "Lord, to whom shall we go? You have the words of eternal life; and we have believed, and have come to know, that you are the Holy One of God" (John 6:60–69).

Another incident that is not as shameful as having disciples leave is that of having one's disciples ignore pleas for support. This we find in the Synoptic accounts of Jesus in Gethsemane before his arrest. He informs his disciples of his state of mind, but they blissfully ignore him, opting for sleep instead (read Mark 14:32–42; Matt. 26:36–46; Luke 22:39–46). Eventually at Jesus' arrest the disciples do abandon Jesus. Only John 19:25–26 speaks of anyone of Jesus' in-group near the cross!

SUMMARY WINDOW

The preceding episodes emphasize Mediterranean-Judean concepts of honor and shame. We learn how these are pivotal values in Mediterranean-Judean society. Honor is a claim to worth that is publicly acknowledged. Shame results when a claim to worth is publicly rejected. One's honor rating is of the utmost importance in the first-century Mediterranean, like a credit rating is in the United States today.

Honor and shame are qualities of individuals as well as of groups. An in-group is invariably considered honorable by its members. Males are expected to defend their honor and that of their group when they are challenged. And societal members likewise feel free and honored to defend the honor of eminent social superiors, especially of God.

FOR FURTHER READING

Augsburger, David W. *Pastoral Counseling Across Cultures*. Philadelphia: Westminster Press, 1986. See especially 111–143 on the primary control emotions: anxiety that intimidates, shame that suppresses, and guilt that represses (and their opposites: boasting, honor, and innocence).

Gilmore, David D., ed. *Honor and Shame and the Unity of the Mediterranean*. Washington: American Anthropological Association, 1987. A valuable series of essays with full bibliography.

Malina, Bruce J. *The New Testament World: Insights from Cultural Anthropology*. 2d edition. Louisville, Ky.: Westminster/John Knox Press, 1993. See especially chapter 2 on honor and shame.

Malina, Bruce J., and Jerome H. Neyrey. "Honor and Shame in Luke-Acts: Pivotal Values of the Mediterranean World." In *The Social World of Luke-Acts: Models for Interpretation*, edited by Jerome H. Neyrey. Peabody, Mass.: Hendrickson, 1991, 25–65.

Moxnes, Halvor. "Honor and Righteousness in Romans." *Journal for the Study of the New Testament* 32 (1988): 61–77.

Moxnes, Halvor. "Honor, Shame, and the Outside World in Paul's Letter to the Romans." In *The Social World of Formative Christianity and Judaism*, edited by Jacob Neusner. Philadelphia: Fortress Press, 1988, 207–218.

II

GENERAL INTERPERSONAL BEHAVIOR

INTRODUCTORY WINDOW

This set of episodes outlines the general standards that govern interpersonal behavior in first-century Israel. The ancient Mediterranean was an extremely interpersonally intensive society. Those institutions and situations that allowed for a maximum of interpersonal interaction were favored over those institutions and situations that allowed for privacy or aloneness. The principle in vogue, then, was a maximum of personal interaction and a minimum of social isolation.

Sources of information that permitted people to carry on without asking information from another were usually not available or were available only at appreciable cost. For example, there were extremely few books, rarely any signs listing prices although some listed tolls, and no regular advertisements. And whatever was available for reading had to be read aloud or announced by a herald. Since reading alone was a clear instance of isolation, and isolation was to be avoided, there was little incentive for literacy.

Like other Mediterraneans, ancient Judeans interacted with each other at an intense level. Their language was intimate and their emotions were openly expressed—in contrast to the behavior of Americans. Furthermore, Judeans employed a set of criteria for evaluating people that differed from the criteria followed by Americans. Perhaps the main difference is that Mediterraneans judge others according to socially shared stereotypes, while Americans generally judge others in terms of psychological motives and individualistic stories.

Effeminate Males?

A number of American soldiers were sitting around discussing some of the experiences they had had during their first week in first-century Palestine. They all agreed that they thought Jerusalem had some beautiful sights and that the surrounding scenery with the sea nearby and the contrasting desert and hills everywhere was lovely. Several mentioned that they often saw men going arm-in-arm or hand-in-hand with other men, while women did the same with other women. They laughed at a few remarks made by one of the men, but they were not sure how this behavior shown by the Judeans should be interpreted.

How should such behavior be interpreted?

MEANINGS IN WINDOW 8

Why Jesus Is Tactile

Behavior such as males walking arm-in-arm or hand-in-hand illustrates the greater degree to which ancient Judean friends feel they can enter each other's personal boundaries. Generally, friendships involve a far greater lowering of social and psychosocial boundaries in the first-century Mediterranean than in the contemporary United States. Friends express their relationships to others more openly, often by touching. To walk hand-in-hand or arm-in-arm announces to others that this is my friend; any difficulty you cause him will require that you answer to me as well. Such behavior is not unusual. There is a positive value to touching in Mediterranean society, ancient and modern. Males will hold hands, lock arms, and generally poke at each other much more frequently than in the United States. It is part of the great value attached to being included in the boundaries of another. This same perception of lowered or no boundaries can be seen in the appropriateness of friends walking into one another's houses at any time, of handling one another's books or other goods without asking permission and the like. There is no sexual connotation to touching except, as in America, in the case of heterosexual touching (e.g., see the idiom for sexual relations in 1 Cor. 7:1: "to touch a woman"; "woman" was the ordinary word for a married woman, a wife; see also Matt. 5:28: looking at a "woman" lustfully means looking at a married woman, hence with a view to adultery, which dishonors the husband).

The best-known New Testament scene of such Mediterranean tactileness is in John's Gospel:

One of his disciples, whom Jesus loved, was lying close to the breast of Jesus; so Simon Peter beckoned to him and said, "Tell us who it is of whom he speaks." So lying thus, close to the breast of Jesus, he said to him, "Lord, who is it?" Jesus answered, "It is he to whom I shall give this morsel when I have dipped it." So when he had dipped the morsel, he gave it to Judas, the son of Simon Iscariot. Then after the morsel, Satan entered into him. Jesus said to him, "What you are going to do, do quickly" (John 13:23–27).

Other New Testament examples of tactileness refer largely to healing scenes. Touching the garment of the healer puts one in the social space, hence power area, of the healer. Similarly, the healer touches the sick person, symbolizing a sharing of space, the health-giving with the ill, as well as a sharing of the healer's power and solidarity. Finally, recall Paul's injunction, surely mirroring prevailing custom, "Greet one another with a holy kiss" (Rom. 16:16; 1 Cor. 16:20; 2 Cor. 13:12; also 1 Thess. 5:26).

Open-hearted, Close-minded?

Moshe ben Bulba had met a number of Americans who had come to first-century Palestine and had become good friends with several of them. One evening at a party for both Mediterranean Judeans and Americans, Moshe was asked what he thought was the main difference between Mediterranean Judeans and Americans. Moshe replied that Mediterranean Judeans wear their hearts inside out and keep their minds locked, while Americans do the opposite. Most of the people there thought this was an excellent metaphor.

What is the meaning of Moshe's metaphor?

Why Jesus Is So Emotional

Mediterraneans are more openly emotional than Americans. Furthermore, they generally do not attempt to justify and/or explain their emotions, while Americans often feel obliged to make such attempts. Mediterranean Judeans, like all Mediterraneans, value spontaneity in feeling and action. Hence, they openly express their emotions. Americans, on the other hand, tend to be more reserved, partially because of the value of restraint (inherited from Northern Europe) and partially because emotional display is considered childish. This does not mean, however, that all Americans are reserved and no Mediterranean Judeans are restrained. These are simply the most dominant patterns within the two cultures. However, they are not the only patterns.

The show of emotion is an attribute of the honorable man in the ancient Mediterranean. Thus we read that Caesar pronounced a eulogy for his young wife (which was unusual since this was usually done only for older women) resulting in popular sympathy "so that they were fond of him, as a man who was gentle and full of feeling" (Plutarch, *Lives: Caesar* V 2, Loeb 451). Caesar burst into tears when reading and thinking about Alexander's kingship as a youth (*ibid.*, XI 3, Loeb 469), and he wept at the death of his mortal enemy Pompey (*ibid.*, XLVIII 2, Loeb 555). Similarly, "Cato was the only one to commend his course [Pompey's], and this from a desire to spare the lives of his fellow citizens; for when he saw even those of the enemy who had fallen in the battle, to the number of a thousand, he burst into tears, muffled up his head, and went away" (*ibid.*, XLI 1, Loeb 543). Finally, when Cicero took leave of his brother, "after embracing one another and weeping aloud, they parted" (Plutarch, *Lives: Cicero* XLVII 2, Loeb 203). Males read and write poetry (along with the poems in the Bible, note, for example, how Alexander the Great often sponsored poetry contests, mentioned by Plutarch, *Life of Alexander*, IV 6 666, Loeb 231–233; XXIX 1 681, Loeb 309). They are not expected to be too logical. They embrace and kiss in public (Matt. 26:48 and parallels; Luke 7:45; Acts 20:37; Rom. 16:16; etc.) and speak of their emotional attachment to each other (Phil. 1:8; Christians are urged to be emotionally attached to each other: Eph. 4:32; Phil. 2:1; 1 Peter 3:8). Women are considered to be coldly practical (see Proverbs 31, cited in Meanings in Window 29).

Herod (Matt. 2:16), Jesus' fellow villagers in Nazareth (Luke 4:28), the ten against James and John (Matt. 20:24), the chief priests and scribes (Matt. 21:15), and Jesus himself (Mark 10:14) are described as indignant, that is, showing displeasure, losing composure, for some reason or other. Paul's letter to the Galatians fits this category as well.

The Gospels of Matthew and Mark frequently inform us about Jesus' being emotionally moved by people in distress: the leaderless crowds (Matt. 9:36); the crowd (Mark 6:34; Matt. 9:36); the famished people (Mark 8:2; Matt. 15:32); two blind men (Matt. 20:34; Mark 9:22 is a bit different). Luke says the same thing only about Jesus' encounter with the widow of Nain (Luke 7:13).

Finally, a parade of examples of the features in this Window are to be seen in the famous episode of Jesus at Lazarus' tomb:

> Now Jesus had not yet come to the village, but was still in the place where Martha had met him. When the Jews who were with her in the house, consoling her, saw Mary rise quickly and go out, they followed her, supposing that she was going to the tomb to weep there. Then Mary, when she came where Jesus was and saw him, fell at his feet, saying to him, "Lord, if you had been here, my brother would not have died." When Jesus saw her weeping, and the Jews who came with her also weeping, he was deeply moved in spirit and troubled; and he said, "Where have you laid him?" They said to him, "Lord, come and see." Jesus wept. So the Jews said, "See how he loved him!" (John 11:30–36).

Hot-tempered?

Chris Simon was sitting in one of the parks in Tiberias reading his paper and enjoying the lovely day. While he was sitting there, two Mediterranean Judeans came along and sat next to him on the bench.

After about five minutes an argument started between the two Mediterranean Judeans. Since Chris understood some Aramaic, he realized that they were arguing over a relatively unimportant decision at a sporting match. The argument, however, increased in intensity with the men pushing each other and being abusive. Chris thought that surely they would come to blows. However, the argument seemed to end abruptly, and one of the men asked the other to come and have a drink with him. They left the park together, talking as if nothing had occurred.

How can the behavior of the Mediterranean Judeans be understood?

<u>MEANINGS IN WINDOW 10</u>

The New Testament and Specific Emotions

Interestingly enough, in first-century Palestine, as in the modern Mediterranean, different emotional states are expected to be accompanied by specific behavior patterns. The arguing that Chris witnessed was an instance of the way in which anger provokes, maintains, and supports specific behavior (and vice versa). In other words, Mediterranean-Judeans' reactions to emotional states are more specific than are Americans'. Thus, while Americans could reflect anger in several ways, Mediterranean Judeans would reflect it in only a fairly specific fashion.

Emotions are less diffuse than in American experience, and more specific to specific situations accompanying specific actions. For example: (a) Jealousy inevitably leads to anger. Axiomatically, Proverbs 6:34 states:

> For jealousy makes a man furious,
> and he will not spare when he takes revenge.

(See also Num. 5:29–30; 25:11; Deut. 29:20; 32:16, 21–23; Ps. 78:58; Ezek. 5:13; 16:38, 42; 36:5; 38:19; Zech. 8:2; 2 Cor. 12:20.)

(b) Grief also leads to anger:

> At two things my heart is grieved,
> and because of a third anger comes over me:
> a warrior in want through poverty,
> and intelligent men who are treated contemptuously;

a man who turns back from righteousness to sin—
the Lord will prepare him for the sword! (Sir. 26:28 [19]).

A similar sequence is found in Mark 3:5: "And he looked around at them with anger, grieved at their hardness of heart, and said to the man, 'Stretch out your hand.' He stretched it out, and his hand was restored."

(c) Rage, on the other hand, leads to killing:

Then Herod, when he saw that he had been tricked by the wise men, was in a furious rage, and he sent and killed all the male children in Bethlehem and in all that region who were two years old or under, according to the time which he had ascertained from the wise men (Matt. 2:16).

(See also 2 Chron. 16:10; 28:9; Job 39:24; Ps. 46:6; Jer. 46:9; Hos. 11:6.)
Rage is also the emotion proper to battle:

Just as dawn was breaking, the two armies joined battle, the one [of Judas Maccabeus] having as pledge of success and victory not only their valor but their reliance upon the Lord, while the other made rage their leader in the fight (2 Macc. 10:28).

(d) Emotion is so focused that people can either love or hate, with no middle ground. Consider the following statements from the Gospels:

No one can serve two masters; for either he will hate the one and love the other, or he will be devoted to the one and despise the other. You cannot serve God and mammon (Matt. 6:24; Luke 16:31).

If any one comes to me and does not hate his own father and mother and wife and children and brothers and sisters, yes, and even his own life, he cannot be my disciple (Luke 14:26).

He who loves father or mother more than me is not worthy of me; and he who loves son or daughter more than me is not worthy of me (Matt. 10:37).

He who loves his life loses it, and he who hates his life in this world will keep it for eternal life (John 12:25).

(e) Emotional attachment, too, is quite focused, either for or against, with no middle ground:

For he that is not against us is for us (Mark 9:40).

He who is not with me is against me, and he who does not gather with me scatters (Matt. 12:30).

But Jesus said to him, "Do not forbid him; for he that is not against you is for you" (Luke 9:50).

He who is not with me is against me, and he who does not gather with me scatters (Luke 11:23).

What then shall we say to this? If God is for us, who is against us? (Rom. 8:31).

That people violently opposed in argument turn out quite differently in the end is indicated, perhaps, in Mark's Gospel, where Pharisees and Herodians bent on Jesus' death at the outset (Mark 3:6) end up showing admiring astonishment at him (Mark 12:17).

Parents, Students, Teachers

When the parent-teacher association meeting of the Nehemiah Academy in Jerusalem was announced, Frank Lloyd knew he must attend. Frank had been teaching English at the school for only two months. This would be his first meeting with his students' parents. He knew that the school was highly selective so he was looking forward to meeting some of the Mediterranean-Judean parents.

When he got to the meeting, he was immediately put on the defensive. A number of parents came up and inquired why their sons had not been doing well in his class. A few of the parents were even rude. They said things such as "I know my child is bright and if he got a D on your test then there must be something wrong with your teaching," or "Why do you dislike my child so much?" Frank was glad when the meeting was over.

How would you account for the "rude" behavior of the Mediterranean-Judean parents?

MEANINGS IN WINDOW 11

Why Jesus Emphasizes Doing

As previously noted, standards used to evaluate people in the ancient (and modern) Mediterranean world are quite different from those used by people in the United States. When it comes to passing judgment on some activity, Americans focus on what a person does, how the person performs the task at hand. Frank's pattern of grading reflected this very American tendency. In first-century Palestine, judgment is based on the character of the person, as well as on his performance. In fact, the two criteria are intertwined to such an extent in first-century Palestine that a bad performance is seen as indicative of bad character and vice versa. A grade, therefore, is considered an assessment of one's personhood as well as of one's performance. A grade of "C" means the person is a "C"-quality person—and did "C" work on the test.

Furthermore, in first-century Palestine, poor performance in school is thought to reflect faulty upbringing. There is a direct relationship between parentage (and parenting) and performance by offspring. Given this information, the anger of the parents is quite understandable. Finally, there is a strong tendency for Mediterranean Judeans to blame others for their own faults. Frank served as a sort of scapegoat for the Mediterranean-Judean parents. Thus there are a range of reasons explaining their reactions.

29

Thus some Mediterranean perspectives include the ideas that bad performance equals bad character, poor performance outside the home reflects faulty upbringing, and our shortcomings are never really our fault, so let's find the true culprit—a scapegoat to blame for our shortcomings.

In this regard notice the emphasis on performance, on doing, to reveal character in the series of parables at the close of the Sermon on the Mount:

> You will know them by their fruits. Are grapes gathered from thorns, or figs from thistles? So, every sound tree bears good fruit, but the bad tree bears evil fruit. A sound tree cannot bear evil fruit, nor can a bad tree bear good fruit. Every tree that does not bear good fruit is cut down and thrown into the fire. Thus you will know them by their fruits.
>
> Not every one who says to me, "Lord, Lord," shall enter the kingdom of heaven, but he who does the will of my Father who is in heaven. On that day many will say to me, "Lord, Lord, did we not prophesy in your name, and cast out demons in your name, and do many mighty works in your name?" And then will I declare to them, "I never knew you; depart from me, you evildoers."
>
> Every one then who hears these words of mine and does them will be like a wise man who built his house upon the rock; and the rain fell, and the floods came, and the winds blew and beat upon that house, but it did not fall, because it had been founded on the rock. And every one who hears these words of mine and does not do them will be like a foolish man who built his house upon the sand; and the rain fell, and the floods came, and the winds blew and beat against that house, and it fell; and great was the fall of it (Matt. 7:16–27).

And note the advice in John: "If you know these things, blessed are you if you do them" (John 13:17).

Performance Isn't Everything

Two teachers at a local grade school in Bethlehem decided to teach one of their courses jointly. One of the teachers, Amir, was a Judean and the other, Bill, was an American. They both gave lectures to the students and jointly presented the information to be mastered.

They also prepared, administered, and graded the examination that was given to the students at the end of the year. Up to this point everything had gone very smoothly between the two men, but when it came to assigning grades, a number of problems arose. Bill would look at the scores that a particular student had and then assign him a grade. Amir also assigned grades and at the end they compared their results. It turned out that Amir's grades were much higher than Bill's, and they had many difficulties making final evaluations.

Bill would say, "Look, Amir, this boy has received C's on all of his tests and should therefore get a C." Amir would counter, "But he's such a good boy, and he told me that he has difficulties with the type of test we gave."

They were finally able to give grades, but Bill decided never again to attempt a joint course with a Mediterranean-Judean teacher.

How would you account for the discrepancy between the grades that Bill gave and the grades that Amir gave?

Why Jesus Judged More than Performance

Mediterranean Judeans and Americans generally use different standards for evaluating people. Americans tend to evaluate people in task situations solely on the basis of their performance. This is reflected in Bill's desire to grade the students on the basis of their test scores only. In first-century Judea, judgment is based on the character of the person, as well as his performance. A grade is an assessment of the person as well as of the person's performance. Thus, the fact that the student was such a good person, was immersed in personal difficulties, was a well-meaning person, and the like influenced Amir's grading. In other words, Americans learn to judge essentially by task fulfillment, by performance, by what a person has done and actually does. Mediterraneans judge by both performance and character.

For example, consider the parable of the Prodigal Son. By U.S. standards, the older son is quite correct and has every right to be irate. But by Mediterranean standards, the younger son is treated fairly:

31

There was a man who had two sons; and the younger of them said to his father, "Father, give me the share of property that falls to me." And he divided his living between them. Not many days later, the younger son gathered all he had and took his journey into a far country, and there he squandered his property in loose living. And when he had spent everything, a great famine arose in that country, and he began to be in want. So he went and joined himself to one of the citizens of that country, who sent him into his fields to feed swine. And he would gladly have fed on the pods that the swine ate; and no one gave him anything. But when he came to himself he said, "How many of my father's hired servants have bread enough and to spare, but I perish here with hunger! I will arise and go to my father, and I will say to him, 'Father, I have sinned against heaven and before you; I am no longer worthy to be called your son; treat me as one of your hired servants.'" And he arose and came to his father. But while he was yet at a distance, his father saw him and had compassion, and ran and embraced him and kissed him. And the son said to him, "Father, I have sinned against heaven and before you; I am no longer worthy to be called your son." But the father said to his servants, "Bring quickly the best robe, and put it on him; and put a ring on his hand, and shoes on his feet; and bring the fatted calf and kill it, and let us eat and make merry; for this my son was dead, and is alive again; he was lost, and is found." And they began to make merry.

Now his elder son was in the field; and as he came and drew near to the house, he heard music and dancing. And he called one of the servants and asked what this meant. And he said to him, "Your brother has come, and your father has killed the fatted calf, because he has received him safe and sound." But he was angry and refused to go in. His father came out and entreated him, but he answered his father, "Lo, these many years I have served you, and I never disobeyed your command; yet you never gave me a kid, that I might make merry with my friends. But when this son of yours came, who has devoured your living with harlots, you killed for him the fatted calf!" And he said to him, "Son, you are always with me, and all that is mine is yours. It was fitting to make merry and be glad, for this your brother was dead, and is alive; he was lost, and is found" (Luke 15:11–32).

Similarly, within this perspective consider the parable in Matthew 21:

"What do you think? A man had two sons; and he went to the first and said, 'Son, go and work in the vineyard today.' And he answered, 'I will not'; but afterward he repented and went. And he went to the second and said the same; and he answered, 'I go, sir,' but did not go. Which of the two did the will of his father?" They said: "The first." Jesus said to them: "Truly, I say to you, the tax collectors and the harlots go into the kingdom of God before you" (Matt. 21:28–31).

Alone Means with a Group

Harley Johnston was a student studying classics at the University of Jerusalem for a year. He got to know a lot of the Mediterranean-Judean students, exclusively males. Females, he found out, were not allowed to attend the university because of the presence of unattached, unrelated males.

Harley had some difficulty in adjusting to the social patterns. A couple of times he attempted to strike up a friendship with someone and was surprised that when he would go to see the person, there might be two or three other people there who would join the person. The same thing also happened when Harley would go to visit a male classmate to study or chat. He would often find that there were other people and no work would get done. He did not quite understand what was going on.

What was going on?

Group Aloneness in the Gospels

In first-century Palestine, people tend to be very group-oriented in their dealings with each other. Mediterranean Judeans generally do not place as high a value on privacy in the American sense of being alone or being alone with another person. Consequently, they feel quite free to drop in on their friends unannounced, no matter how many others are there—and whenever they so desire. This ready openness to have others join the group is perhaps indicative of the greater degree of lack of social boundaries between and among Mediterranean-Judean friends as compared to the social boundaries that exist among American friends. While Mediterranean Judeans generally value privacy far less than Americans do, the concept is not totally alien to their culture. But privacy is usually confined to core family matters that might bring dishonor on that unit.

Consider the times when Jesus goes off to be alone in the Gospel story. Almost invariably he is alone with a group, or alone with a crowd within earshot. For example, in the following passages, one is hard pressed to imagine Jesus alone in an American sense:

> And when he was alone, those who were about him with the twelve asked him concerning the parables (Mark 4:10).

> Now it happened that as he was praying alone the disciples were with him; and he asked them, "Who do the people say that I am?" (Luke 9:18).

To be alone or apart or in private usually means to be with one's circle of close friends or within one's family, that is, apart from the general public. Thus to be in a small group with one's fictive kin or close associates, even twelve or more of them, leaves one in private. Consider the following:

> He did not speak to them without a parable, but privately to his own disciples he explained everything (Mark 4:34).

> And taking him aside from the multitude privately, he put his fingers into his ears, and he spat and touched his tongue (Mark 7:33).

> And when he had entered the house, his disciples asked him privately, "Why could we not cast it out?" (Mark 9:28).

> And as he sat on the Mount of Olives opposite the temple, Peter and James and John and Andrew asked him privately . . . (Mark 13:3).

> Then turning to the disciples he said privately, "Blessed are the eyes which see what you see!" (Luke 10:23).

> Therefore whatever you have said in the dark shall be heard in the light, and what you have whispered in private rooms shall be proclaimed upon the housetops (Luke 12:3).

Yet there are instances where the words "alone," "apart," or "privately" sufficiently describe privacy in the American sense. For example:

> If your brother sins against you, go and tell him his fault, between you and him alone. If he listens to you, you have gained your brother (Matt. 18:15).

Still, one may doubt the total absence of others, since "privately" may involve a large group:

> I went up by revelation; and I laid before them (but privately before those who were of repute) the gospel which I preach among the Gentiles, lest somehow I should be running or had run in vain (Gal. 2:2).

Age Counts More than Youth

Hank and Zev were working together at a small business in Jericho. Both men were in their early twenties. One afternoon, Josue ben Hara, their boss, came in and asked Zev to do some research for him at a nearby government agency. Zev went to the agency, told them he came to obtain some information on behalf of his boss, and that he was a college graduate. The person in charge refused to allow Zev to retrieve the information, telling him he was too young to have access to such sources. The next time Zev took an older staff member with him and got permission to do the work. Hank was surprised by all of this.

Why did Zev get permission to do the work when he took an older staff member along?

Respect for Older Persons

The older staff member gave Zev the status needed to get the cooperation of those at the government agency. One of the factors determining status in first-century Palestine is age. Generally, the older the individual is, the higher his or her status as evaluated by others. Thus, even though Zev was qualified by education, he did not have the status needed to gain the cooperation of those at the agency because he was not old enough. By bringing the older staff member along, his status was raised and he was able to do his research.

The older an individual is, the higher the status. Hence youth will always have difficulty with credibility. Listen to Sirach on this topic:

> If you are willing, my son, you will be taught,
>   and if you apply yourself you will become clever.
> If you love to listen you will gain knowledge,
>   and if you incline your ear you will become wise.
> Stand in the assembly of the elders.
>   Who is wise? Cleave to him (Sir. 6:32–34).

> Do not disregard the discourse of the aged,
>   for they themselves learned from their fathers;
> because from them you will gain understanding
>   and learn how to give an answer in time of need (Sir. 8:9).

> You have gathered nothing in your youth;
>   how then can you find anything in your old age?

35

What an attractive thing is judgment in gray-haired men,
    and for the aged to possess good counsel!
How attractive is wisdom in the aged,
    and understanding and counsel in honorable men!
Rich experience is the crown of the aged,
    and their boast is the fear of the Lord (Sir. 25:3–6).

Speak, you who are older, for it is fitting that you should,
    but with accurate knowledge (Sir. 32:3).

While in 1 Corinthians Paul notes that people might have difficulty with Timothy, in 1 Timothy we find out that the difficulty was Timothy's youth:

When Timothy comes, see that you put him at ease among you, for he is doing the work of the Lord, as I am. So let no one despise him. Speed him on his way in peace, that he may return to me; for I am expecting him with the brethren (1 Cor. 16:10–11).

Let no one despise your youth, but set the believers an example in speech and conduct, in love, in faith, in purity (1 Tim. 4:12).

The "Friendly" Teacher

A young American teacher, Les White, came to first-century Palestine to spend two years teaching English in a Mediterranean-Judean academy. He visited the school a few times before he started teaching in order to see how those teachers conducted their classes.

Les decided that the Mediterranean-Judean teachers were far too formal with their students, so he conducted his classes in a very different manner. He would enter the room informally dressed and then ask the students if they had any problems with their homework. Whenever a discussion occurred, he would laugh and joke with the students. After the homework was discussed, he would move on to new material. He soon found, however, that the class was getting unruly. Students would talk amongst themselves during class, show up late for class, and not do their work. Les wondered what he had done wrong.

Why did the class become unruly?

MEANINGS IN WINDOW 15

A World of Formality in Private and in Public

Les was not formal enough. In first-century Palestine and in the modern Mediterranean, a certain amount of formality is expected of one's superiors. That is, a certain gap or boundary must exist between superior and subordinate. Because Les treated his class so informally, he lost status in the eyes of his students. Thus, they did not feel that it was necessary to follow his orders any longer. The ideal situation would be to maintain status while showing concern and genuine interest in the lives and efforts of the students.

Consider the attitude revealed in the following passage:

> And Paul, looking intently at the council, said, "Brethren, I have lived before God in all good conscience up to this day." And the high priest Ananias commanded those who stood by him to strike him on the mouth. Then Paul said to him, "God shall strike you, you whitewashed wall! Are you sitting to judge me according to the law, and yet contrary to the law you order me to be struck?" Those who stood by said, "Would you revile God's high priest?" And Paul said, "I did not know, brethren, that he was the high priest; for it is written, 'You shall not speak evil of a ruler of your people' "(Acts 23:1–5).

A certain amount of formality is expected of one's superiors with a resulting distance between superiors and social subordinates. It was for not showing due respect to the high priest that Jesus was dishonored with a slap at his interrogation:

> The high priest then questioned Jesus about his disciples and his teaching. Jesus answered him, "I have spoken openly to the world; I have always taught in synagogues and in the temple, where all Jews come together; I have said nothing secretly. Why do you ask me? Ask those who have heard me, what I said to them; they know what I said." When he had said this, one of the officers standing by struck Jesus with his hand, saying, "Is that how you answer the high priest?" Jesus answered him, "If I have spoken wrongly, bear witness to the wrong; but if I have spoken rightly, why do you strike me?" (John 18:19–23).

Paul articulates the socially required formality with his injunction:

> Let every person be subject to the governing authorities. For there is no authority except from God, and those that exist have been instituted by God. . . . Therefore one must be subject, not only to avoid God's wrath but also for the sake of conscience" (Rom. 13:1, 5).

And he concludes with a sort of general principle:

> Pay all of them their dues, taxes to whom taxes are due, revenue to whom revenue is due, respect to whom respect is due, honor to whom honor is due (Rom. 13:7).

The same sort of formality gap is expected in Christian groups:

> But we beseech you, brethren, to respect those who labor among you and are over you in the Lord and admonish you (1 Thess. 5:12).

The various injunctions to be subject are similarly about proper formalities: wives to husbands, children to parents, slaves to owners (see, e.g., Eph. 5:21–6:9; Col. 3:18–24). As 1 Peter says,

> Be subject for the Lord's sake to every human institution, whether it be to the emperor as supreme, or to governors as sent by him to punish those who do wrong and to praise those who do right (1 Peter 2:13–14).

Furthermore, informal teacher-student, master-disciple relations do not exist as a rule. Note how throughout the Gospels, Jesus is addressed with a title, both by his disciples and by others. The titles "Lord" (equivalent to "Sir" and "Master," distance indicators of respect) and "Teacher" (a recognition of a status role) are the most common. The point is that there are no informal relations between Jesus and anyone else in the Gospel narrative.

For master, see Matthew 26:25, 49; Mark 9:5; 11:21; 14:45 (translating *Rabbi*); Luke 5:5; 8:24, 45; 9:33, 49 (translating *epistates*). For teacher see Matthew 8:19; 12:38; 17:24; 19:16; 22:16, 24, 36; 26:18; Mark 4:38; 5:35; 9:17, 38; 10:17, 20, 35; 12:14, 19, 32; 13:1; 14:14; Luke 3:12; 7:40; 8:49; 9:38; 10:25; 11:45; 12:13; 18:18; 19:39; 20:21, 28, 39; 21:7; 22:11.

The "Friendly" Mistress

Lauren Boulay's husband had been working in first-century Palestine for about five years. The couple bought a house and, because she helped her husband six days a week, she had a maid come in to clean and do the washing and ironing. Lauren treated the maid as a friend and paid her well.

Each morning she would leave out the clothes she wanted cleaned and ironed. When she returned, however, she discovered that her Mediterranean-Judean maid would only do certain dresses or blouses. When Lauren inquired why this was so, the maid replied that she didn't think a certain dress was attractive or that it was too early to wear sleeveless blouses. Lauren was very angry.

Why did the maid act this way?

The Social Dimensions of Christian Service

The maid is testing Lauren to see what she can get away with. In first-century Palestine, maids generally have relatively low status. Many are slaves, the lowest status in the social system. As a result, they more or less expect that their employer or owner will be formal with them. By treating the maid like a friend and thus not maintaining the needed gap or distance between her and the maid, Lauren gave the impression that her status was also relatively low. As a result, the maid began to disobey Lauren and was in effect trying to see how far she could go.

To treat a servant or a slave like a friend is to fail to maintain the needed social gap between oneself and the servant. This gives the clear impression that one's status is also as low as that of the servant.

> Fodder and a stick and burdens for an ass;
>   bread and discipline and work for a servant.
> Set your slave to work, and you will find rest;
>   leave his hands idle, and he will seek liberty.
> Yoke and thong will bow the neck,
>   and for a wicked servant there are racks and tortures.
> Put him to work, that he may not be idle,
>   for idleness teaches much evil.
> Set him to work, as is fitting for him,
>   and if he does not obey, make his fetters heavy.
> Do not act immoderately toward anybody,
>   and do nothing without discretion.

If you have a servant, let him be as yourself,
  because you have bought him with blood.
If you have a servant, treat him as a brother,
  for as your own soul you will need him.
If you ill-treat him, and he leaves and runs away,
  which way will you go to seek him? (Sir. 33:25–31).

Do not be ashamed . . .
  of whipping a wicked servant severely (Sir. 42:1, 5).

And we have this advice from Christian supervisors:

Servants, be submissive to your masters with all respect, not only to the kind and gentle but also to the overbearing (1 Peter 2:18).

Bid slaves to be submissive to their masters and to give satisfaction in every respect; they are not to be refractory (Titus 2:9).

And note the problem that arises for Peter when Jesus washes the feet of his apostles (recorded only in John's Gospel). Jesus' behavior is that of a slave.

[Jesus] arose from supper, laid aside his garments, and girded himself with a towel. Then he poured water into a basin, and began to wash the disciples' feet, and to wipe them with the towel with which he was girded. He came to Simon Peter; and Peter said to him, "Lord, do you wash my feet?" Jesus answered him, "What I am doing you do not know now, but afterward you will understand." Peter said to him, "You shall never wash my feet." Jesus answered him, "If I do not wash you, you have no part in me." Simon Peter said to him, "Lord, not my feet only but also my hands and my head!" Jesus said to him, "He who has bathed does not need to wash, except for his feet, but he is clean all over; and you are clean, but not every one of you." For he knew who was to betray him; that was why he said, "You are not all clean."
  When he had washed their feet, and taken his garments, and resumed his place, he said to them, "Do you know what I have done to you? You call me Teacher and Lord; and you are right, for so I am. If I then, your Lord and Teacher, have washed your feet, you also ought to wash one another's feet" (John 13:4–14).

In its turn, the Synoptic tradition has the following:

But Jesus called them to him and said, "You know that the rulers of the Gentiles lord it over them, and their great men exercise authority over them. It shall not be so among you; but whoever would be great among you must be your servant, and whoever would be first among you must be your slave; even as the Son of man came not to be served but to serve, and to give his life as a ransom for many" (Matt. 20:25–28).

Among Mediterraneans, there is a strong tendency to resent people with superior status who fail to act in a manner appropriate to that status. By supervising subordinates, superiors maintain boundaries and win respect.

To gain respect in the Christian community, Christian supervisors (bishops) must act appropriately at home. They must manage their own households well, keeping their children "submissive and respectful in every way" (1 Tim. 3:4).

The wise are to maintain appropriate gravity of behavior:

> The heart of the wise is in the house of mourning;
>   but the heart of fools is in the house of mirth (Eccl. 7:4).

A Seller's Market

After coming to first-century Palestine, it was necessary for Tom Sanders to purchase assorted furniture for his new apartment. He bought most of this merchandise from local Mediterranean-Judean merchants and was relatively pleased with his purchases.

About a month later he was entertaining a friend of his who had been in the country a number of years. He mentioned where he had bought the things and how much they had cost. His friend was amazed. He told Tom that he had paid 30 percent more than he should have paid on each of the items. Tom protested and said that he had paid what the merchant asked. He had checked at other places and had been quoted similar prices. He was very, very angry.

Why did the friend tell Tom he had paid too much?

Fairness Is Status-specific

Tom was not aware that it is the custom in first-century Palestine to bargain over prices. In first-century Palestine, prices are usually not marked at all. If they are marked, they are intentionally marked higher. The reason for this is that life in the Mediterranean is interpersonally intensive. Here the merchant and customer are expected to bargain. Bargaining is a way of life in first-century Palestine, and merchants feel cheated if they do not get to bargain with their customers. It is almost a ceremonial procedure. The outcome is a fair price. However, in traditional Mediterranean society, a fair price is a price that befits the social status of the buyer. In the United States, on the other hand, a fair price is one that befits the market value of the item for sale.

Haggling or bargaining with a view to finding the proper social price is equally evidenced in the Bible. Of course the best-known example is Abraham's haggling with God over the fate of Sodom and Gomorrah:

> Then the LORD said, "Because the outcry against Sodom and Gomorrah is great and their sin is very grave, I will go down to see whether they have done altogether according to the outcry which has come to me; and if not, I will know."
>
> So the men turned from there, and went toward Sodom; but Abraham still stood before the LORD. Then Abraham drew near, and said, "Wilt thou indeed destroy the righteous with the wicked? Suppose there are fifty righteous within the city; wilt thou then destroy the place and not spare it for the fifty righteous who are in it? Far be it from thee to do such a thing, to slay the righteous with the wicked, so that the righteous fare as the wicked! Far be that from thee! Shall not

the Judge of all the earth do right?" And the LORD said, "If I find at Sodom fifty righteous in the city, I will spare the whole place for their sake." Abraham answered, "Behold, I have taken upon myself to speak to the Lord, I who am but dust and ashes. Suppose five of the fifty righteous are lacking? Wilt thou destroy the whole city for lack of five?" And he said, "I will not destroy it if I find forty-five there." Again he spoke to him, and said, "Suppose forty are found there." He answered, "For the sake of forty I will not do it." Then he said, "Oh let not the Lord be angry, and I will speak. Suppose thirty are found there." He answered, "I will not do it, if I find thirty there." He said, "Behold, I have taken upon myself to speak to the Lord. Suppose twenty are found there." He answered, "For the sake of twenty I will not destroy it." Then he said, "Oh let not the Lord be angry, and I will speak again but this once. Suppose ten are found there." He answered, "For the sake of ten I will not destroy it." And the LORD went his way, when he had finished speaking to Abraham; and Abraham returned to his place (Gen. 18:20–33).

Of course the true social situation for haggling is trade. Job speaks of traders haggling over an enslaved person: "Will traders bargain over him? Will they divide him up among the merchants?" (Job 41:6). And Proverbs describes the line of the buyer, depreciating goods to gloat over a good buy later: "'It is bad, it is bad,' says the buyer; but when he goes away, then he boasts" (Prov. 20:14).

Sirach warns against a good buy that ends up really costing more: "There is a man who buys much for a little, but pays for it seven times over" (Sir. 20:12).

However, the rule everywhere and always was: "Buyer beware!" Again, Sirach warns: "A merchant can hardly keep from wrongdoing, and a tradesman will not be declared innocent of sin" (Sir. 26:29). Cheating by using false balances or scales seems to have been prevalent at certain periods (see Amos 8:5–6; Hos. 12:7). Hence Sirach advises that one need not be ashamed of profit from dealing with merchants (Sir. 42:5).

Jesus, on the other hand, urges merchants to be honest and desist from swearing to bolster the value of their merchandise. The oaths cited by Jesus were in fact used by merchants and traders:

Again you have heard that it was said to the men of old, "You shall not swear falsely, but shall perform to the Lord what you have sworn." But I say to you, Do not swear at all, either by heaven, for it is the throne of God, or by the earth, for it is his footstool, or by Jerusalem, for it is the city of the great King. And do not swear by your head, for you cannot make one hair white or black. Let what you say be simply "Yes" or "No"; anything more than this comes from evil (Matt. 5:33–37).

In sum, consider Sirach's warning about whom not to seek advice from, and note where he situates the haggling opponents:

Do not consult with a woman about her rival
    or with a coward about war,
with a merchant about barter
    or with a buyer about selling,

with a grudging man about gratitude
   or with a merciless man about kindness,
with an idler about any work
   or with a man hired for a year
      about completing his work,
with a lazy servant about a big task—
   pay no attention to these in any matter of counsel (Sir. 37:11).

SUMMARY WINDOW

The preceding episodes illustrate the rather intensive nature of interpersonal behavior in first-century Palestine. We also saw how Mediterranean Judeans tend to express their emotions more openly than Americans. Certain expressions (like crying) reflect specific emotional states, much in the way that certain behaviors reflect specific positions within a status hierarchy. Finally, we saw how Mediterranean Judeans often allow a person's character to influence their judgments of his performance, while Americans rarely do this.

FOR FURTHER READING

For more information on this area, largely from the Eastern Mediterranean, see:

Abu-Hilal, Ahmad. "Arab and North-American Social Attitudes: Some Cross-Cultural Comparisons." *Mankind* 22 (1982): 193–207.

Malina, Bruce J. "Dealing with Biblical (Mediterranean) Characters: A Guide for U.S. Consumers." *Biblical Theology Bulletin* 19 (1989): 127–141.

Malina, Bruce J. "Is There a Circum-Mediterranean Person: Looking for Stereotypes." *Biblical Theology Bulletin* 22 (1992): 66–87.

Sharabi, Hisham, with Mukhtar Ani. "Impact of Class and Culture on Social Behavior: The Feudal Bourgeois Family in Arab Society." In *Psychological Dimensions of Near Eastern Studies*, edited by L. Carl Brown and Norman Itzkowitz. Princeton, N.J.: Darwin Press, 1977, 240–256.

Triandis, Harry C. "Cross-Cultural Studies on Individualism and Collectivism." In *Nebraska Symposium on Motivation, 1989: Cross-Cultural Perspectives* (Current Theory and Research in Motivation 37), edited by John J. Berman. Lincoln, Neb.: University of Nebraska Press, 1990, 41–133.

III

IN-GROUP

INTRODUCTORY WINDOW

The in-group–out-group distinction is one of the most central features of Mediterranean culture. Among other aspects, what makes this distinction significant is the moral assessment of persons that it marks off. The in-group, rooted in kinship and its extensions (friendship, workmates, patronage, and the like), is always to be supported, respected, and given loyalty. The out-group, all other persons, simply does not count. Often the out-group may be treated as a different species. A distinction such as that between Israel and the other nations (= Gentiles), or between Judeans and other nations (= Gentiles) points to the in-group–out-group distinction.

This next set of Windows focuses on the quality of the in-group. It is important to realize that in-group–out-group boundaries are forever shifting. While kinship points to rigid in-group–out-group markings, the lines are rather malleable and can be redrawn in varying situations. However, such kaleidoscoping boundaries are tolerably predictable although Americans find such redrawing confusing. The Windows presented here underscore the flexibility Mediterraneans evidence in reading the distinction.

A Friend of a Friend

Louis Lubush checked into his hotel near the Damascus Gate in Jerusalem and went out for a short walk and a snack. After a few hours he returned to his hotel and, after asking a few questions at the desk, returned to his room. The next morning, after breakfast at the roof restaurant and a brief stop at the desk, he went to his office. On the way to work, Louis found himself pondering the fact that a lot of the Mediterranean Judeans he had met seemed so aloof. At the office one of his colleagues mentioned that he was a very good friend of Yitzhak ben Dudah, the manager of the hotel. He insisted that Louis mention this fact to Mr. ben Dudah. When Louis returned, he asked for Mr. ben Dudah and told him of his contact with their mutual friend. For the next ten days that Louis stayed at the hotel, he was surprised at the almost suffocatingly warm treatment he received from all the hotel personnel.

Why did the Mediterranean Judeans change their behavior toward Louis so abruptly after he told Mr. ben Dudah of their mutual friend?

MEANINGS IN WINDOW 18

Recommendations in Early Christianity

By telling the hotel manager of their mutual acquaintance, Louis was regarded as a friend by Mr. ben Dudah. Mention of a mutual friend served to make Louis no longer a stranger but rather a friend of the manager. Louis was treated better because Mediterranean Judeans will usually attempt to help a friend whenever and however possible. The system works by networking with friends of friends of friends. Tipping in such circumstances would be to no effect since money rarely buys anything personal within the in-group. Surely tipping has no real impact on service. In sum, the mention of a mutual friend makes one a friend of a friend, hence a friend.

Friends of friends were quite significant in early Christian travel arrangements. Third John is a letter of recommendation, as is Paul's letter to Philemon. All the letters of Ignatius of Antioch, a Christian bishop martyred about A.D. 106, are about making travel arrangements with the help of Christian friends. Within Paul's epistles we find various words of recommendation as well:

> I commend to you our sister Phoebe, a deaconess of the church at Cenchreae, that you may receive her in the Lord as befits the saints, and help her in whatever she may require from you, for she has been a helper of many and of myself as well (Rom. 16:1–2).

When Timothy comes, see that you put him at ease among you, for he is doing the work of the Lord, as I am. So let no one despise him. Speed him on his way in peace, that he may return to me; for I am expecting him with the brethren (1 Cor. 16:10–11).

I hope in the Lord Jesus to send Timothy to you soon, so that I may be cheered by news of you. I have no one like him, who will be genuinely anxious for your welfare. They all look after their own interests, not those of Jesus Christ. But Timothy's worth you know, how as a son with a father he has served with me in the gospel. I hope therefore to send him just as soon as I see how it will go with me; and I trust in the Lord that shortly I myself shall come also.

I have thought it necessary to send to you Epaphroditus my brother and fellow worker and fellow soldier, and your messenger and minister to my need, for he has been longing for you all, and has been distressed because you heard that he was ill. Indeed he was ill, near to death. But God had mercy on him, and not only on him but on me also, lest I should have sorrow upon sorrow. I am the more eager to send him, therefore, that you may rejoice at seeing him again, and that I may be less anxious. So receive him in the Lord with all joy; and honor such men, for he nearly died for the work of Christ, risking his life to complete your service to me (Phil. 2:19–30).

Tychicus will tell you all about my affairs; he is a beloved brother and faithful minister and fellow servant in the Lord. I have sent him to you for this very purpose, that you may know how we are and that he may encourage your hearts, and with him Onesimus, the faithful and beloved brother, who is one of yourselves. They will tell you of everything that has taken place here. Aristarchus my fellow prisoner greets you, and Mark the cousin of Barnabas (concerning whom you have received instructions—if he comes to you, receive him) (Col. 4:7–10).

Neighbors

Having noticed that his baby crib needed painting, Lenny went to a number of nearby hardware stores in Caesarea. He tried to get non-toxic paint but was unable to find any. Later in the week, as he was leaving for work one morning, he asked his Mediterranean-Judean next-door neighbor if he knew where he could get the paint. His neighbor inquired about why it was needed and Lenny told him.

When he returned from work late that afternoon, he found his neighbor sitting on the driveway at work on the crib. He noticed that his neighbor had sanded down the crib before painting it and had obviously done a lot of work. Lenny tried to take over the job at this point, but his neighbor refused. Later, after having thanked his neighbor very much, Lenny tried to pay him for the paint he had purchased, but his neighbor refused to take it. Lenny was a little embarrassed by all of this.

Why did the neighbor paint the crib and refuse any money afterward?

MEANINGS IN WINDOW 19

What Is a Neighborhood?

Lenny and the neighbor were friends. The neighbor was only acting as a true friend and expected no remuneration. The neighbor thought of Lenny as a member of his in-group. As a result, he felt it his duty to aid Lenny in every way possible. Neighbors who are friends are in-group members (see the previous Window). This emphasis on the in-group–oriented social dimensions of life is most vividly illustrated by the Mediterranean attitude toward space and the planning of residential quarters. Dale F. Eickleman, in *The Middle East: An Anthropological Approach*, has noted that even a small town might have thirty to forty neighborhoods or quarters in the perception of its residents. One's neighborhood or quarter consists of households

> claiming multiple personal ties and common interests based on varying combinations of kinship, common origin, ethnicity, patronage and clientship, participation in factional alliances and spatial propinquity itself. . . . Only those clusters of households evaluated as sustaining a particular quality of life are known as quarters. . . . Component households in a quarter assume that they share a certain moral unity so that in some respects social space in their quarter can be regarded as an extension of their own households. This closeness is symbolized in a number of ways: the exchange of visits on feast days, assistance and participation in the activities connected with births, circumcisions, weddings, and funerals of component

households, and the like. . . . Because of the multiple ties which link the residents of a quarter, respectable women who never venture to the main market can circulate discreetly within their quarter, since the residents all assume a closeness to each other (106–107).

The point is that houses put together in a section of town do not form a neighborhood or city/town quarter. Residential space is not principally in terms of physical landmarks but in a shared concept of the social order. Perceptions and assessments of the spatial order are rooted in and follow one's understanding of how people are situated and relate to each other; that is the social order.

Thus for Jesus to have a house in Capernaum is indicative of where his network of in-group relations was constituted. The first persons he calls to take part in his movement are from there. And that they so quickly respond is indicative of the in-group network there (see Mark 1 and parallels).

Friendly or Nosey?

Lois Barr, a school teacher at the American school in first-century Jerusalem, was amazed at the questions that were asked her by Mediterranean Judeans whom she considered to be only casual acquaintances. When she left her apartment or returned to it, people would ask her where she was going or where she had been. If she stopped to talk, she was asked questions like, "How old are you?" or "How much do you make a month?" or "Where did you get that dress you are wearing?" She thought the Mediterranean Judeans were very rude.

Why did the Mediterranean Judeans ask Lois such "personal" questions?

Who Is a Neighbor?

The casual acquaintances were acting as friends do in first-century Palestine although Lois did not realize it. It is not improper for people living in the same village or neighborhood to consider each other members of an in-group, and in-group members freely ask these questions of one another. Furthermore, these questions reflect the fact that interpersonal relationships, even casual ones, tend to involve a far greater lowering of social and psychological boundaries in first-century Palestine than in North America. As a result, neighbors and acquaintances are generally free to ask questions that would seem too personal in America.

Chances are they already knew Lois' network of affiliations. Remember, whether or not some information is personal depends on the cultural cues concerning who has a right to such information. In this case, the Mediterranean Judeans did not consider these questions too personal since they felt they had a right to know their neighbor and potential in-group member.

Perhaps this is a good time to consider the meaning of "neighbor" in the Gospels. The term refers to a social role with rights and obligations that derive simply from living close with others—the same village or neighborhood. Neighbors of this sort are an extension of one's kin group. The neighbor is a person with whom one has daily, face-to-face contact: "Do not plan evil against your neighbor who dwells trustingly beside you" (Prov. 3:29). The cultivation and maintenance of good relations with a neighbor has been the common sense advice inculcated by traditional wisdom, for "better is a neighbor who is near than a brother who is far away" (Prov. 27:10). If one is sensible, one will not commit adultery with his neighbor's wife (Prov. 6:29), nor will one speak evil of or belittle one's neighbor (Prov. 11:9, 12). One will not act violently with one's neighbor (Prov. 16:29). And one will not take a neighborly argument to a wider audience (Prov. 25:9), bear false witness against one's neighbor (Prov. 25:18), deceive one's neighbor (Prov. 26:19), or flatter one's neighbor (Prov. 27:14; 29:5).

But to move in on a neighbor and invade his personal space as though he were a member of your family will distance him and lead to his detached unconcern: "Let your foot be seldom in your neighbor's house, lest he become weary of you and hate you" (Prov. 25:17). Sirach offers similar advice.

However, in times of need one may impose upon one's neighbor as one would on one's kin. For example, Jesus said:

> Which of you who has a friend will go to him at midnight and say to him, "Friend, lend me three loaves; for a friend of mine has arrived on a journey, and I have nothing to set before him"; and he will answer from within, "Do not bother me; the door is now shut, and my children are with me in bed; I cannot get up and give you anything"? I tell you, though he will not get up and give him anything because he is his friend, yet because of his importunity he will rise and give him whatever he needs (Luke 11:5–8).

And one gives daily greeting, asking after the welfare of a neighbor. This point is implied in typical behavior noted in the contrast:

> You have heard that it was said, "You shall love your neighbor and hate your enemy." But I say to you, Love your enemies and pray for those who persecute you, so that you may be sons of your Father who is in heaven; for he makes his sun rise on the evil and on the good, and sends rain on the just and on the unjust. For if you love those who love you, what reward have you? Do not even the tax collectors do the same? And if you salute only your brethren, what more are you doing than others? Do not even the Gentiles do the same? You, therefore, must be perfect, as your heavenly Father is perfect (Matt. 5:43–48).

These scenarios point to daily interaction. However, first-century Judeans likewise knew that all Israel were neighbors. The injunction of Leviticus 19:18 to love one's neighbor as oneself applied to the whole house of Israel, whether the injunctions were actually carried out or not. It is to clarify this point that the parable of the Good Samaritan is presented with the conclusion that a neighbor is one in deed, one who has compassion on another:

> But he, desiring to justify himself, said to Jesus, "And who is my neighbor?" Jesus replied, "A man was going down from Jerusalem to Jericho, and he fell among robbers, who stripped him and beat him, and departed, leaving him half dead. Now by chance a priest was going down that road; and when he saw him he passed by on the other side. So likewise a Levite, when he came to the place and saw him, passed by on the other side. But a Samaritan, as he journeyed, came to where he was; and when he saw him, he had compassion, and went to him and

bound up his wounds, pouring on oil and wine; then he set him on his own beast and brought him to an inn, and took care of him. And the next day he took out two denarii and gave them to the innkeeper, saying, 'Take care of him; and whatever more you spend, I will repay you when I come back.' Which of these three, do you think, proved neighbor to the man who fell among the robbers?" (Luke 10:29–36).

Unknown Friends

An American and a Mediterranean Judean who were old friends were working together on a project of mutual interest. In the middle of their conversation, a messenger came to the Mediterranean-Judean gentleman and told him that his wife had fallen down a staircase and was at a nearby hospital. The American offered to take his friend to see his wife, so they stopped off at the house to pick up some of her personal things and then drove to the hospital.

Upon reaching their destination, they discovered that official visiting hours were only in the morning, and the guard refused to let them enter. After a rather heated argument, the Mediterranean-Judean gentleman gave up and handed the guard the package of personal effects and asked him to deliver it to his wife. The guard inquired about the wife's name. Upon learning the family name, he seemed quite surprised and asked the man where he was from. He told the guard that he was originally from a certain village and the guard smiled and let them enter. The American was somewhat puzzled by the guard's change in behavior.

How would you explain the guard's behavior?

MEANINGS IN WINDOW 21

Love as Group Attachment

By virtue of having come from the same village, the hospital guard and the Mediterranean-Judean husband were at this time in the same in-group. In-group members were expected to make allowances and take risks for one another, even at great personal cost. Allowing the husband to enter was a perfectly reasonable risk on the part of the Mediterranean-Judean guard, who could have been severely reprimanded or punished by the hospital administrator. However, the guard did not know that the husband was an in-group member until he mentioned his village of origin.

The whole set of exhortations in early Christian writings according to which Christians should love and/or serve one another points to an attempt on the part of leadership to help people from varying social levels to realize they are now all in-group. To love means to remain practically attached to the group, to act like an in-group member. The reason for the frequent exhortations is that old in-group ties die very slowly in strongly group-oriented societies. Christians must now feel free to do favors for each other as much as they did for old in-group relations.

The new commandment of John's Gospel is well known:

A new commandment I give to you, that you love one another; even as I have loved you, that you also love one another. By this all men will know that you are my disciples, if you have love for one another (John 13:34–35).

(The new commandment is also found in John 15:12, 17 and frequently in 1 John 3:11, 23; 4:7, 11, 12; 2 John 5.)

The tradition is as old as Paul, where it initially looked to the in-group with concern about obtaining respect from the majority out-group:

And may the Lord make you increase and abound in love to one another and to all men, as we do to you (1 Thess. 3:12).

But concerning love of the brethren you have no need to have any one write to you, for you yourselves have been taught by God to love one another (1 Thess. 4:9).

In general only in-group interaction is in view here as well as in documents from other early Christian communities:

Love one another with brotherly affection; outdo one another in showing honor (Rom. 12:10).

Owe no one anything, except to love one another; for he who loves his neighbor has fulfilled the law (Rom. 13:8).

Finally, brethren, farewell. Mend your ways, heed my appeal, agree with one another, live in peace, and the God of love and peace will be with you (2 Cor. 13:11).

For you were called to freedom, brethren; only do not use your freedom as an opportunity for the flesh, but through love be servants of one another (Gal. 5:13).

With all lowliness and meekness, with patience, forbearing one another in love (Eph. 4:2).

We are bound to give thanks to God always for you, brethren, as is fitting, because your faith is growing abundantly, and the love of every one of you for one another is increasing (2 Thess. 1:3).

And let us consider how to stir up one another to love and good works (Heb. 10:24).

Having purified your souls by your obedience to the truth for a sincere love of the brethren, love one another earnestly from the heart (1 Peter 1:22).

Above all hold unfailing your love for one another, since love covers a multitude of sins (1 Peter 4:8).

Greet one another with the kiss of love.
　　Peace to all of you that are in Christ (1 Peter 5:14).

Landlords and Tenants

Larry and Deb Tout were looking for a house to rent in Jerusalem. They would be stationed there for at least two years, so they decided it would be best to find a house. They got a list of houses that were available from the newspaper and decided to go about the city and look at a few of them. At their first stop they were warmly greeted, and although they did not like the house, they were more or less forced to have a cool drink before they left. They thought that the people were nice to be so kind, but they really had to be on their way. They found at the next house, however, that they were treated the same way, with the Mediterranean Judeans insisting that they come in and have a drink before leaving. They found that they only saw a small number of the places that they had originally wanted to see. All in all they were quite upset at the end of the day since they thought they wasted lots of time socializing.

Why were the Touts treated so warmly wherever they went?

The Householder and Tenant Relationship

Because there is a relatively long-term relationship between landlord and renter, Mediterranean Judeans desire this relationship to be friendly. That is, they would like the relationship to become one between in-group members. Also, the Touts are Americans, and Mediterranean Judeans are usually very hospitable to foreigners when personal contact is first initiated.

It is important to note the difference between American entertainment of friends and visitors and hospitality in the ancient world. Hospitality was not about entertaining family and friends. Rather hospitality meant the receiving of strangers into one's care, into one's intimate in-group, and shielding the stranger with one's honor. After the stay the stranger left as enemy or friend. While with a host, a stranger was embedded in the host, so to speak. It was up to the host to look to the needs of the guest, even to the point of defending the guest's honor with his (the host's) own life. Furthermore, there were no real equivalents of modern hotels or motels in the ancient world. Places for travelers were all of dubious moral quality. As for physical amenities, these inns were geared more for the maintenance of donkeys and camels than persons. Hence the need for hospitality, that is, for receiving strangers.

The culture provided implicit rules for strangers and hosts to follow. Without going into these now, it is important to realize that early Christian exhortations to hospitality were aimed at sedentary Christians, directing them to receive traveling fellow Christians and to admit them into the local in-group:

Now in the neighborhood of that place were lands belonging to the chief man of the island, named Publius, who received us and entertained us hospitably for three days (Acts 28:7).

Contribute to the needs of the saints, practice hospitality (Rom. 12:13).

Now a bishop must be above reproach, the husband of one wife, temperate, sensible, dignified, hospitable, an apt teacher. . . . (1 Tim. 3:2).

And she [the widow] must be well attested for her good deeds, as one who has brought up children, shown hospitality, washed the feet of the saints, relieved the afflicted, and devoted herself to doing good in every way (1 Tim. 5:10).

[The bishop must be] hospitable, a lover of goodness, master of himself, upright, holy, and self-controlled (Titus 1:8).

Do not neglect to show hospitality to strangers, for thereby some have entertained angels unawares (Heb. 13:2).

Practice hospitality ungrudgingly to one another (1 Peter 4:9).

Boss or Patron?

Pat Jacobs had read a lot about the Mediterranean-Judean culture before coming to first-century Palestine to set up a branch of his company. Two weeks after he arrived and hired a number of workers, he gave a party for his Mediterranean-Judean employees. At the plant he insisted that his workers call him "Mr. Jacobs," and that they realize he was the boss. And so at the party, while he related to his employees rather formally, he still went around and talked to as many of them as he could. Then, too, every day on the job, he did his best to indicate his concern for the welfare of his employees.

After three months, his auditors did their first accounting and found the business to be doing extremely well. When a number of Pat's American friends heard how the business was doing, they were truly surprised to hear about how well things were going after only three months in Jerusalem.

Why was Pat doing so well after only three months?

MEANINGS IN WINDOW 23

About Gifts and Favors, Divine and Human

Pat was acting toward his employees as a Mediterranean employer should. Thus the Mediterranean Judeans were happy and worked hard for him. The employer-employee relationship is much more personal in first-century Palestine than in the United States. By giving the party for his employees and showing concern for each of them, Pat was meeting the Mediterranean-Judean expectations of what a good boss should be like. Hence, the employees placed him within their in-group and worked hard for him. Although being friendly, Pat still managed to maintain a distance from the employees. This enabled him to keep their respect and to maintain his status while showing concern.

The employer-employee relationship is much more personal in first-century Palestine than in the United States. A good boss is a patron, one who treats an employee as a surrogate or substitute father would, with concern for the employee and his family and ready to do favors should the employee need them. In return, the employer has the loyalty of his employees and the honor that comes from such employees. The same formal distance as existed between a father and older son is kept with favored employees. But there is no requirement that employees be favored.

The only requirement is that employees be paid promptly on the day of their service; thus the traditional legislation in Deuteronomy 24:14–15 and Leviticus 19:13, and articulated in the tradition:

> Do not hold over till the next day the wages of any man who works for you, but pay him at once; and if you serve God you will receive payment (Tobit 4:14).

> To take away a neighbor's living is to murder him;
> to deprive an employee of his wages is to shed blood (Sir. 34:22).

These daily wages were not a favor but a debt. They do not come from patronage but from justice:

> Now to one who works, his wages are not reckoned as a gift but as his due (Rom. 4:4).

> For the laborer deserves his wages (Luke 10:7).

> For the scripture says, "You shall not muzzle an ox when it is treading out the grain," and, "The laborer deserves his wages" (1 Tim. 5:18).

However, favors could be added to wages:

> Then my (Tobit's) wife Anna earned money at women's work. She used to send the product to the owners. Once when they paid her wages, they also gave her a kid; and when she returned to me it began to bleat. So I said to her, "Where did you get the kid? It is not stolen, is it? Return it to the owners; for it is not right to eat what is stolen." And she said, "It was given to me as a gift in addition to my wages" (Tobit 2:11–14).

The same patronal addition or favor is found in the famous parable of the hirelings, describing God's patronage in Matthew 20:1–16 (quoted on page 157).

The traditional problem was that employers defrauded their workers. They either delayed payment or did not pay at all. See Jeremiah 22:13–16; Malachi 3:5; and in the New Testament:

> Behold, the wages of the laborers who mowed your fields, which you kept back by fraud, cry out; and the cries of the harvesters have reached the ears of the Lord of hosts (James 5:4).

On the other hand, to hire oneself out for wages was considered socially negative. Wage laborers were low-status persons, held in low esteem. Consider the following stereotypes:

> Has not man a hard service upon earth,
> and are not his days like the days of a hireling?
> Like a slave who longs for the shadow,
> and like a hireling who looks for his wages,

so I am allotted months of emptiness,
    and nights of misery are apportioned to me (Job 7:1–3).

Do not consult . . .
with a man hired for a year about completing his work (Sir. 37:11).

He who is a hireling and not a shepherd, whose own the sheep are not, sees the wolf coming and leaves the sheep and flees; and the wolf snatches them and scatters them. He flees because he is a hireling and cares nothing for the sheep (John 10:12–13).

And yet, there were faithful hired hands. Consider this lineup from Sirach:

Do not exchange a friend for money,
    or a real brother for the gold of Ophir.
Do not deprive yourself of a wise and good wife,
    for her charm is worth more than gold.
Do not abuse a servant who performs his work faithfully,
    or a hired laborer who devotes himself to you.
Let your soul love an intelligent servant;
    do not withhold from him his freedom (Sir. 7:18–21).

Townmates

Uri was from the village of Modain and grew up there. Elliott, an American friend, had spent some time with him in his home village. He had noticed the rather fierce confrontations between various groups in the village. Yet when Elliott and Uri were in Jerusalem, Elliott noticed that when anyone from Modain showed up at Uri's place of business, Uri was inclined to do everything he could for anyone from his home village, even for people who were definitely members of some village "out-group," not very friendly with his family.

How can Uri's behavior be understood?

In Israel Versus in Christ as In-Group

When in Jerusalem, the only people with whom Uri had any common ties were others from Modain. Hence, he regarded them as in-group members and treated them accordingly. The boundaries of the in-group were constantly shifting. Thus, when in Modain, certain villagers were with Uri's in-group and others were not. However, when in Jerusalem, the old boundaries did not apply. All people from Modain were within his in-group there.

The boundaries of the in-group are constantly shifting in first-century Christian writings as well. The geographical division of the house of Israel in the first century was Judea, Perea, and Galilee. What all the residents with allegiance to the Jerusalem Temple had in common was birth into the same people, the house of Israel. But this group quickly broke into three in-groups: the Judeans, Pereans, and Galileans. Jesus was not a Judean but a Galilean, as were his disciples. It was Judeans who put Jesus the Galilean to death. And all of these geographically based groups had their countless subgroups, with various and changing loyalties. According to the story, Jesus shifted from the tiny hamlet of Nazareth, to the much larger village of Capernaum (see Mark 2:1, where Jesus of Nazareth was at home).

On the other hand, to outsiders, all these in-groups fused into one, the Judeans. Paul sees himself as an Israelite, of the tribe of Benjamin. Yet in the larger Roman world, he came from Tarsus and lived according to Judean customs, called Judaism, with allegiance to the God of Israel in Jerusalem in Judea. Most such emigrant Judeans never expected to move back to Judea. They remained either resident aliens or citizens in the places of their birth, yet were categorized by the geographical location of their original ethnic roots.

The reason for this was that the main way for categorizing living beings—animals and humans—in the first-century Mediterranean was by geographical place of ethnic origin (not place of birth). Beings of similar geographical place of origin were to harbor in-group feelings even if long departed from that place of origin. And that place of origin endowed group members with particular characteristics.

In the book of Acts, when Paul begins his travels, he heads for local synagogues, basically community centers, in the lands between Jerusalem and Rome. At these synagogues he finds in-group members who likewise follow the customs of Judea, even centuries after their families left the place of their ethnic origin. It is this in-group affiliation in the northeast corner of the Mediterranean basin that allows for the initial spread of an alternate version of Israelite ideology called "The Way." Thus,

> they passed on from Perga and came to Antioch of Pisidia. And on the sabbath day they went into the synagogue and sat down. After the reading of the law and the prophets, the rulers of the synagogue sent to them, saying, "Brethren, if you have any word of exhortation for the people, say it." . . .
>
> And when the meeting of the synagogue broke up, many Jews and devout converts to Judaism followed Paul and Barnabas, who spoke to them and urged them to continue in the grace of God (Acts 13:14–15, 43).

> Now at Iconium they entered together into the [Judean] synagogue, and so spoke that a great company believed, both of [Judeans] and of Greeks (Acts 14:1).

> Now when they had passed through Amphipolis and Apollonia, they came to Thessalonica, where there was a synagogue of the [Judeans] (Acts 17:1).

> The brethren immediately sent Paul and Silas away by night to Beroea; and when they arrived they went into the [Judean] synagogue (Acts 17:10).

> So he argued in the synagogue with the [Judeans] and the devout persons, and in the market place every day with those who chanced to be there (Acts 17:17).

> And he argued in the synagogue every sabbath, and persuaded [Judeans] and Greeks (Acts 18:4).

> And he left there and went to the house of a man named Titius Justus, a worshiper of God; his house was next door to the synagogue. Crispus, the ruler of the synagogue, believed in the Lord, together with all his household; and many of the Corinthians hearing Paul believed and were baptized (Acts 18:7–8).

> And they all seized Sosthenes, the ruler of the synagogue, and beat him in front of the tribunal. But Gallio paid no attention to this. . . .
>
> . . . And they came to Ephesus, and he left them there; but he himself went into the synagogue and argued with the [Judeans] (Acts 18:17, 19).

> He began to speak boldly in the synagogue; but when Priscilla and Aquila heard him, they took him and expounded to him the way of God more accurately (Acts 18:26).

And he entered the synagogue and for three months spoke boldly, arguing and pleading about the kingdom of God (Acts 19:8).

Jesus set up his faction by recruiting core members with the invitation: "Follow me." They, of course, expected something in return for joining his group. Consider the responses to Peter's question as given in the triple Synoptic tradition:

Peter began to say to him, "Lo, we have left everything and followed you." Jesus said, "Truly, I say to you, there is no one who has left house or brothers or sisters or mother or father or children or lands, for my sake and for the gospel, who will not receive a hundredfold now in this time, houses and brothers and sisters and mothers and children and lands, with persecutions, and in the age to come eternal life" (Mark 10:28–30).

Then Peter said in reply, "Lo, we have left everything and followed you. What then shall we have?" Jesus said to them, "Truly, I say to you, in the new world, when the Son of man shall sit on his glorious throne, you who have followed me will also sit on twelve thrones, judging the twelve tribes of Israel. And every one who has left houses or brothers or sisters or father or mother or children or lands, for my name's sake, will receive a hundredfold, and inherit eternal life" (Matt. 19:27–29).

And Peter said, "Lo, we have left our homes and followed you." And he said to them, "Truly, I say to you, there is no man who has left house or wife or brothers or parents or children, for the sake of the kingdom of God, who will not receive manifold more in this time, and in the age to come eternal life" (Luke 18:28–30).

Trust or Competence?

Wes Bond was studying the operations and working procedures of a number of Mediterranean-Judean businesses and noticed quite a few things that intrigued him. One procedure that seemed to occur in all the firms was that the boss seemed to have one or two trusted employees who did personal favors for him and always seemed to be in the know. It was obvious, however, that these men were not necessarily the most competent nor were they in positions that were particularly powerful. Upon further inquiry it turned out that these people were usually relatives or from the same village as the boss. Hmm, thought Wes, a type of nepotism!

Why, in all the Mediterranean-Judean firms, did the boss have only one or two trusted employees?

MEANINGS IN WINDOW 25

Jesus, In-Groups, and Core Groups

Mediterranean Judeans generally trust only in-group members. This is very common in first-century Palestine. Since relatives, for the most part, are automatically within the central in-group and are, therefore, highly trusted, they are often placed in positions of trust by the boss. Also, since it is expected that one will help his in-group member first before anyone else, the employer's relatives are often placed in high positions even though others may have greater ability.

Note how in Acts, James the brother of the Lord (Acts 12:17; 15:12–14; see also Gal. 1:19) turns out to be the central personage in the Christian community of Jerusalem. The Gospel story offers no indication of his being in the ranks of Jesus' disciples. Further, he himself was presumably among those who came to take Jesus home because people were saying: "He is beside himself" (Mark 3:21). For Jesus' family in this episode, consider: "'Is not this the carpenter, the son of Mary and brother of James and Joses and Judas and Simon, and are not his sisters here with us?' And they took offense at him" (Mark 6:3; Matt. 13:55). And yet this James ends up head of the Jerusalem church.

And note how the three core disciples—Peter, John, and James—form an in-group with Jesus and are thus frequently cited together:

> And he allowed no one to follow him except Peter and James and John the brother of James (Mark 5:37; Luke 8:51).

And after six days Jesus took with him Peter and James and John, and led them up a high mountain apart by themselves; and he was transfigured before them (Mark 9:2; Matt. 17:1; Luke 9:28).

And as he sat on the Mount of Olives opposite the temple, Peter and James and John and Andrew asked him privately (Mark 13:3).

And he took with him Peter and James and John, and began to be greatly distressed and troubled (Mark 14:33).

Because of in-group cohesion in the culture, the biggest obstacle facing prospective members of the various Jesus groups was their families. Besides pointing up trouble with his own family (as in Mark 3:31–35 and parallels), the tradition ascribes the following words to Jesus:

Do not think that I have come to bring peace on earth; I have not come to bring peace, but a sword. For I have come to set a man against his father, and a daughter against her mother, and a daughter-in-law against her mother-in-law; and a man's foes will be those of his own household (Matt. 10:34–36).

Do you think that I have come to give peace on earth? No, I tell you, but rather division; for henceforth in one house there will be five divided, three against two and two against three; they will be divided, father against son and son against father, mother against daughter and daughter against her mother, mother-in-law against her daughter-in-law and daughter-in-law against her mother-in-law (Luke 12:51–53).

Prospective Friends

Eddie McMahon was stationed outside Jerusalem. After living there a number of years, one fine day he observed a lovely Mediterranean-Judean young woman and decided to marry her. So he set in motion the process that would lead to eventual marriage. He found a go-between to negotiate for the young woman with her parents. During the formal engagement period, he got to know her family very well, especially her thirty-six-year-old brother. He was always surprised at the way his prospective brother-in-law would do things for him. For example, once in the space of six weeks, he washed and waxed Eddie's car twice without being asked.

Why did Eddie's prospective brother-in-law do so many things for him?

Jesus and Friends of Friends

Since Eddie is going to marry the Mediterranean-Judean's sister, the brother-in-law feels that Eddie will be a member of the family. In becoming a member of the family, Eddie is also entering the family's in-group. It is expected in first-century Palestine that one helps in-group members whenever and however possible. This does not mean, of course, that such frequent help will always be given, but it is not uncommon.

This incident of a future brother-in-law helping his brother-in-law-to-be is not unlike Jesus healing Peter's mother-in-law almost right after he summons Peter to follow him. The significant item in the passage is that according to Matthew and Mark, Jesus takes the initiative to heal her:

> And when Jesus entered Peter's house, he saw his mother-in-law lying sick with a fever; he touched her hand, and the fever left her, and she rose and served him (Matt. 8:14–15).

> And immediately he left the synagogue, and entered the house of Simon and Andrew, with James and John. Now Simon's mother-in-law lay sick with a fever, and immediately they told him of her. And he came and took her by the hand and lifted her up, and the fever left her; and she served them (Mark 1:29–31).

Luke has the normal description of Jesus as healer. In that view Jesus never heals anyone without someone asking him to do so. So here in Luke:

> He arose and left the synagogue, and entered Simon's house. Now Simon's mother-in-law was ill with a high fever, and they besought him for her. And he stood over her and rebuked the fever, and it left her; and immediately she rose and served them (Luke 4:38–39).

Friends Feel Obligated

Reston lived in first-century Palestine for a number of years and had made friends with many Mediterranean-Judean families. During a party he had one evening, he happened to mention to a few of his Mediterranean-Judean friends that he was moving the following Sunday to a new house, and that he wasn't looking forward to all the work involved in the move. He was amazed on Sunday morning to find that a large number of his Mediterranean-Judean friends had come to help him move.

How would you account for the large turnout of Reston's Mediterranean-Judean friends?

Christian In-Group Support

Reston has acquired an in-group. The members of this group felt an obligation to help him move. Reston's relatively long period of residence in first-century Palestine has provided him with the opportunity to acquire a rather significant in-group. In-group members are expected to put themselves out for one another, and that is why Reston's friends helped him move.

In-group members (neighbors and friends) feel obliged to help each other. Here we might review what was previously said about the meaning of neighbor in Window 18. Consider, likewise, such neighborly behavior among Christians described by the second-century author Lucian, in a work titled *The Passing of Peregrinus* (12–13, Loeb V 13–15). Previously in the story, we learn that Peregrinus of Syria was a person of dubious character acting like a wandering philosopher. He becomes a Christian while in Palestine and is later imprisoned for this. Lucian writes:

> Well, when he had been imprisoned the Christians, regarding the incident as a calamity, left nothing undone in the effort to rescue him. Then, as this was impossible, every other form of attention was shown him, not in any casual way, but with assiduity; and from the very break of day aged widows and orphan children could be seen waiting near the prison, while their officials even slept inside with him after bribing the guards. Then elaborate meals were brought in, and sacred books of theirs were read aloud, and excellent Peregrinus—for he still went by that name—was called by them "the new Socrates."
>
> Indeed, people came even from the cities in Asia sent by the Christians at their common expense, to succor and defend and encourage the hero. They

show incredible speed whenever any such public action is taken; for in no time they lavish their all. So it was then in the case of Peregrinus; much money came to him from them by reason of his imprisonment, and he procured not a little revenue from it. The poor wretches have convinced themselves first and foremost, that they are going to be immortal and live for all time, in consequence of which they despise death and even willingly give themselves into custody, most of them. Furthermore, their first lawgiver [Jesus] persuaded them that they are all brothers of one another after they have transgressed once for all by denying the Greeks' gods and by worshipping that crucified sophist himself and living under his laws. Therefore they despise all things indiscriminately and consider them common property, receiving such doctrines traditionally without any definite evidence.

SUMMARY WINDOW

In this section, the in-group–out-group distinction was introduced. Mediterraneans, ancient and modern, view the world as composed of offsetting binary groups: we and they, in-group and out-group, for us and against us, human and doubtfully human, and the like. A person's in-group generally consists of the person's family, neighbors, and friends. However, the boundaries of an in-group are quite flexible although the core family in-group abides in spite of any and all alterations.

In-groups can and do change. In-group members are expected to be loyal to each other and to go to great lengths to help each other. In dealings with out-group members, the behavior of ancient Judeans reveals that almost anything goes. While one may be relaxed in dealing with anyone who is in one's in-group, all know that the out-group is full of pitfalls and threats. Care is always required.

FOR FURTHER READING

Banfield, Edward C. *The Moral Basis of a Backward Society*. Glencoe, Ill.: Free Press, 1956.

Eickleman, Dale F. *The Middle East: An Anthropological Approach*. 2d ed. Englewood Cliffs, N.J.: Prentice Hall, 1989.

Triandis, Harry C. and Vasso Vassiliou. "A Comparative Analysis of Subjective Culture." in *Comparative Studies in Behavioral Science: A Wiley Series*, edited by Harry C. Triandis et al. New York: Wiley-Interscience, 1972, 299–301.

IV

INTRA-FAMILY RELATIONS

INTRODUCTORY WINDOW

Mediterranean family structures in antiquity came in varied shapes, called Roman, Greek, and Israelite, among others. However, what all these structures had in common was a gender division of labor. Persons were defined primarily and essentially by their gender and gender roles. These roles were further riveted down by gender definitions of objects (for example, female kitchen utensils, male farm instruments; goats in the female domain, sheep in the male domain), space (kitchen and inside of house, male-free courtyard as female, outside as male), and time (women arrive later and leave first, are not out at night). Children were the concern of mothers, with boys staying with females until about puberty. Fathers had little to do with child rearing. When the boy was thrown into the adult male world, his biggest concern was to behave "like a man," a behavior the child really had little opportunity to observe. Mothers and sons formed the closest bond of affection.

This gender-focused family served as the organizing structure of Mediterranean life. It embodied belongingness, the organizing principle of all Mediterranean societies and a trait of paramount concern to everyone in the culture area (see Windows 1–7 on honor and shame).

Boys and Girls, Not Children

An American and his wife were visiting some friends for the summer in first-century Palestine. During that summer the American's wife had a baby. She was attended to by the local women in Ain Karim, the town where they were staying.

While the husband was waiting for his wife's delivery with some men outside the house, they told him of the local customs relative to childbirth. He was informed that attending women were usually given a gift of some sort by the waiting husband or family when these women announced the birth of a child. And the husband himself recalled seeing a man once give the women a certain amount of money when told of his new-born daughter.

Later on in the day when one of the women came and told him that he was the father of a lovely baby boy, the American was so happy that he gave the attending women an even greater gift than he had once seen the other man give. The woman receiving the gift, however, seemed to react as if he hadn't given enough.

How would you account for the woman's reaction?

MEANINGS IN WINDOW 28

A Gender-divided Society

In first-century Palestine, people do not simply beget and give birth to children. They always generate gender-specific children, and this is the focus of the birth announcement. Boys are viewed as being more important than girls. Consequently, the birth of a boy merits a more significant and expensive gift to the attending women than the birth of a girl. Mediterranean Judeans, like Mediterraneans in general, see the world in terms of gender. The gender division of humankind is used as a basic symbol in terms of which reality is interpreted largely, if not exclusively, as male and female, beginning with the human person. This gender evaluation of the self cuts through such basic areas as groups of family relatives, time, space, and nature.

In the total system, males are considered better simply because they are males; they represent the honor of the group, represent the family to the outside, own everything by means of which the family is viewed by outsiders, and must be ever vigilant about the honor of their women. Women are considered inferior to males, necessarily in need of the protection and care of males, as being the inside of the family, in charge of that area, and as maintaining the family's concern for

72

honor by their chastity. There has always been a tremendous overevaluation of boys within Mediterranean-Judean culture and in the Mediterranean in general. For example, Mediterranean-Judean parents often report how many children they have simply by referring to the number of sons they have.

Statements on the assessment of sons and daughters are not direct in the New Testament. To get an orientation, one might begin by noticing that there are no female birth announcements, that God speaks with women only in a procreative context, that the focal characters are essentially male, and that God is primarily referred to as male or in terms of male roles.

Furthermore, male and female roles, even when they can be unified in a common human term, are often laid out in terms of gender. For example, "Honor your father and your mother" (Deut. 5:16) (not "honor your parents"!); or "What man of you, if his son asks him for bread, will give him a stone?" (Matt. 7:9) (not "if his child"); or "I will be a father to you, and you shall be my sons and daughters" (2 Cor. 6:18) (not children).

Perhaps the most ready source of information about daughters compared with sons is to be found in the so-called Wisdom literature, both in ancient collections such as Psalms and Proverbs and especially in those Israelite writings from the first two centuries before Jesus.

The psalm collection expresses the typical Mediterranean perspective on sons:

> Like arrows in the hand of a warrior
> 	are the sons of one's youth.
> Happy is the man who has his quiver full of them!
> He shall not be put to shame
> 	when he speaks with his enemies in the gate (Ps. 127:4–5).

The only psalm giving information about daughters is the royal wedding song (Psalm 45) in which the king's bride is given the advice all Mediterranean daughters would benefit from:

> Hear, O daughter, consider, and incline your ear;
> 	forget your people and your father's house (Ps. 45:10).

And Ecclesiastes lets slip the commonly held Mediterranean view when he notes the truism that only a son or brother can be counted on:

> A person who has no one, either son or brother, yet there is no end to all his toil, and his eyes are never satisfied with riches, so that he never asks, "For whom am I toiling and depriving myself of pleasure?" This also is vanity and an unhappy business (Eccl. 4:8).

However the clearest expression of the (elite male) attitude toward daughters is that found in Ben Sirach (Ecclesiasticus). The general principle is expressed in Sirach 42:9–11:

A daughter keeps her father secretly wakeful,
    and worry over her robs him of sleep;
when she is young, lest she do not marry,
    or if married, lest she be hated;
while a virgin, lest she be defiled
    or become pregnant in her father's house;
or having a husband, lest she prove unfaithful,
    or, though married, lest she be barren.
Keep strict watch over a headstrong daughter,
    lest she make you a laughingstock to your enemies,
a byword in the city and notorious among the people,
    and put you to shame before the great multitude.

This principle then emerges variously:

Do you have cattle? Look after them;
    if they are profitable to you, keep them.
Do you have children? Discipline them,
    and make them obedient from their youth.
Do you have daughters? Be concerned for their chastity,
    and do not show yourself too indulgent with them.
Give a daughter in marriage; you will have finished a great task.
    But give her to a man of understanding (Sir. 7:22–25).

It is a disgrace to be the father of an undisciplined son,
    and the birth of a daughter is a loss.
A sensible daughter obtains her husband,
    but one who acts shamefully brings grief to her father.
An impudent daughter disgraces father and husband,
    and will be despised by both.
Like music in mourning is a tale told at the wrong time,
    but chastising and discipline are wisdom at all times (Sir. 22:3–6).

Keep strict watch over a headstrong daughter,
    lest, when she finds liberty, she use it to her hurt.
Be on guard against her impudent eye,
    and do not wonder if she sins against you.
As a thirsty wayfarer opens his mouth
    and drinks from any water near him,
so will she sit in front of every post
    and open her quiver to the arrow (Sir. 26:10–12).

However, fathers could be attached to daughters as well as to sons: "He who loves son or daughter more than me is not worthy of me" (Matt. 10:37).

At home daughters usually stay with and help mothers, and when married out, help mothers-in-law. Notice the set of residents in the following scenario from the so-called Q accounts in Matthew and Luke:

For I have come to set a man against his father, and a daughter against her mother, and a daughter-in-law against her mother-in-law (Matt. 10:35).

They will be divided, father against son and son against father, mother against daughter and daughter against her mother, mother-in-law against her daughter-in-law and daughter-in-law against her mother-in-law (Luke 12:53).

It would seem only the married male (husband) and his wife would be spared the division.

Male Tasks, Female Tasks

Ferd Mangelson married a Mediterranean-Judean girl whom he met while stationed in Jerusalem. After the newlyweds were settled in, they decided to have a number of friends over for a party. They invited a good number of their Mediterranean-Judean and American friends over for dinner after sundown on the Sabbath. After everyone had arrived and had a drink, the guests seated themselves for dinner. Ferd got up, and when his wife came in from the kitchen, he said, "Let me come out and help you." He started toward the kitchen door. His wife turned to him in obvious anger and indignation and said, "Be seated, Ferd, it is not your job." Ferd's wife was cool to him the rest of the evening. He couldn't understand why.

Why was Ferd's wife cool to him for the rest of the evening?

Female Roles and Values in the Bible

In offering to help his wife, Ferd was taking on what Mediterranean Judeans would regard as a feminine role. In first-century Palestine, household chores were not the job of the husband; instead, they were the responsibility of the wife. Ferd made the mistake of acting like an American husband rather than a Mediterranean-Judean one. This embarrassed his wife because it occurred in the presence of her friends. The separation of male and female roles within Mediterranean-Judean culture is a significant cultural value.

A typical description of the female role in the household is found at the close of Proverbs:

> A good wife who can find?
>> She is far more precious than jewels.
> The heart of her husband trusts in her,
>> and he will have no lack of gain.
> She does him good, and not harm,
>> all the days of her life.
> She seeks wool and flax,
>> and works with willing hands.
> She is like the ships of the merchant,
>> she brings her food from afar.
> She rises while it is yet night
>> and provides food for her household
>> and tasks for her maidens.

She considers a field and buys it;
    with the fruit of her hands she plants a vineyard.
She girds her loins with strength
    and makes her arms strong.
She perceives that her merchandise is profitable.
    Her lamp does not go out at night.
She puts her hands to the distaff,
    and her hands hold the spindle.
She opens her hand to the poor,
    and reaches out her hands to the needy.
She is not afraid of snow for her household,
    for all her household are clothed in scarlet.
She makes herself coverings;
    her clothing is fine linen and purple.
Her husband is known in the gates,
    when he sits among the elders of the land.
She makes linen garments and sells them;
    she delivers girdles to the merchant.
Strength and dignity are her clothing,
    and she laughs at the time to come.
She opens her mouth with wisdom,
    and the teaching of kindness is on her tongue.
She looks well to the ways of her household,
    and does not eat the bread of idleness.
Her children rise up and call her blessed;
    her husband also, and he praises her:
Many women have done excellently,
    but you surpass them all.
Charm is deceitful, and beauty is vain,
    but a woman who fears the LORD is to be praised (Prov. 31:10–30).

Note that the main quality of a good wife in traditional Mediterranean society is that she works to make the household function well. Good wives are doers, usually at work from morning till night. When faced with a problem, wives (and women) are expected to do something about it, while husbands (and males) sit around contemplating the difficulty.

While Sirach has much to say about wicked wives, he too extols the good wife, describing personal traits rather than the practical:

A wife's charm delights her husband,
    and her skill puts fat on his bones.
A silent wife is a gift of the Lord,
    and there is nothing so precious as a disciplined soul.
A modest wife adds charm to charm,
    and no balance can weigh the value of a chaste soul.
Like the sun rising in the heights of the Lord,
    so is the beauty of a good wife in her well-ordered home.

Like the shining lamp on the holy lampstand,
    so is a beautiful face on a stately figure.
Like pillars of gold on a base of silver,
    so are beautiful feet with a steadfast heart (Sir. 26:13–18).

Finally, in the well-known story of Mary and Martha, note that the problem for Martha is that Mary is behaving like a male, while Martha is duly feminine in being active:

> Now as they went on their way, he entered a village; and a woman named Martha received him into her house. And she had a sister called Mary, who sat at the Lord's feet and listened to his teaching. But Martha was distracted with much serving; and she went to him and said, "Lord, do you not care that my sister has left me to serve alone? Tell her then to help me." But the Lord answered her, "Martha, Martha, you are anxious and troubled about many things; one thing is needful. Mary has chosen the good portion, which shall not be taken away from her" (Luke 10:38–42).

On the other hand, who in the world of Jesus would have been socialized to give precedence to others, to serve others, to rejoice at the successes of others, and the like? Obviously women! By asking his male disciples to take on some of these traits, Jesus does indeed seek to rearrange Mediterranean values.

Parents and Children

Tom Turner, a government representative at the U.S. embassy in first-century Caesarea, was attending his first party at which there were many Mediterranean Judeans. Tom, who was accustomed to this type of party in the United States, engaged in a number of conversations with the local people present at the party. He was somewhat surprised at the fact that in every case, the Mediterranean Judeans he spoke with got around, often quickly, to the topic of their children and their children's accomplishments.

Why did each Mediterranean Judean discuss his children's accomplishments?

The Parents of Sons

The Mediterranean Judeans are very proud of their children largely because of the symbolic meaning they attach to children. Children bear the inherited and acquired status of the parents and their ancestors. In first-century Palestine the behavior of one individual reflects the worth or quality of all his family and friends (which we have called the in-group here). Since parents and children are at the same level of their in-group, the parents will discuss their children's achievements because these achievements are a reflection of the parents' own worth. Thus, if a child has excelled in something, the parents, who are very proud, will want this fact known since it equally means the parents and their group are excelling. The same would be true, proportionately, of discussions about the accomplishments and/or standing of relatives, of village mates, and other friends.

This emphasis on family and in-group puts the good of society almost totally in the background. As a matter of fact Mediterraneans are little concerned about contributing to the overall good of society. Rather their standing relative to other groups in society is of paramount importance. And the quality of their children (as indicated by their accomplishments) is very important to group honor. While the number of male children that a male engenders or begets is quite important to his own honor, it is the quality of children that is at issue here.

The qualities inherent in the children are underscored in the Lukan birth announcements, surely to the glory of the parents. Consider the words to Zechariah, and his words addressed to his forthcoming son:

But the angel said to him, "Do not be afraid, Zechariah, for your prayer is heard,
and your wife Elizabeth will bear you a son, and you shall call his name John.
And you will have joy and gladness,
    and many will rejoice at his birth;
for he will be great before the Lord,
and he shall drink no wine nor strong drink,
and he will be filled with the Holy Spirit,
even from his mother's womb.
And he will turn many of the sons of Israel to the Lord their God,
and he will go before him in the spirit and power of Elijah,
to turn the hearts of the fathers to the children,
and the disobedient to the wisdom of the just,
to make ready for the Lord a people prepared" (Luke 1:13–17).

And you, child, will be called the prophet of the Most High;
for you will go before the Lord to prepare his ways,
to give knowledge of salvation to his people
in the forgiveness of their sins,
through the tender mercy of our God,
when the day shall dawn upon us from on high
to give light to those who sit in darkness and in the shadow of death,
to guide our feet into the way of peace (Luke 1:76–79).

And the words to Mary:

And behold, you will conceive in your womb and bear a son, and you shall call his
name Jesus.
    He will be great, and will be called the Son of the Most High;
    and the Lord God will give to him the throne of his father David,
    and he will reign over the house of Jacob for ever;
    and of his kingdom there will be no end (Luke 1:31–33).

Similarly, note the concern of Jesus' family for their honor in face of the
public assessment of their in-group member as insane:

And when his family heard it, they went out to seize him, for people were saying,
"He is beside himself." . . .
    And his mother and his brothers came; and standing outside they sent to him
and called him. And a crowd was sitting about him; and they said to him, "Your
mother and your brothers are outside, asking for you." And he replied, "Who are
my mother and my brothers?" And looking around on those who sat about him,
he said, "Here are my mother and my brothers! Whoever does the will of God is
my brother, and sister, and mother" (Mark 3:21, 31–35).

A main motive for parents to have their sick children healed has to do with
the quality of the illness and the way it reflects on their honor. Not only were
children intended as insurance in old age but, equally, they mirrored the status
of the family. A demon-possessed child pointed to a defective family, negatively
rating the father as the head of the family.

Consider the following incident. What bothered the father?

And behold, a man from the crowd cried, "Teacher, I beg you to look upon my son, for he is my only child; and behold, a spirit seizes him, and he suddenly cries out; it convulses him till he foams, and shatters him, and will hardly leave him. And I begged your disciples to cast it out, but they could not." Jesus answered, "O faithless and perverse generation, how long am I to be with you and bear with you? Bring your son here." While he was coming, the demon tore him and convulsed him. But Jesus rebuked the unclean spirit, and healed the boy, and gave him back to his father. And all were astonished at the majesty of God (Luke 9:38–43a).

What sort of discipleship required a split in the family in-group? What would the following passage mean to a Mediterranean Judean?

And when they bring you to trial and deliver you up, do not be anxious beforehand what you are to say; but say whatever is given you in that hour, for it is not you who speak, but the Holy Spirit. And brother will deliver up brother to death, and the father his child, and children will rise against parents and have them put to death; and you will be hated by all for my name's sake. But he who endures to the end will be saved (Mark 13:11–13).

Finally, note how the mother and brothers of Jesus are at the upper room with the twelve after the resurrection of Jesus:

And when they had entered, they went up to the upper room, where they were staying, Peter and John and James and Andrew, Philip and Thomas, Bartholomew and Matthew, James the son of Alphaeus and Simon the Zealot and Judas the son of James. All these with one accord devoted themselves to prayer, together with the women and Mary the mother of Jesus, and with his brothers (Acts 1:13–14).

In a short while, a family in-group member takes over as patron or central person among Jesus' followers in Jerusalem. This person was James, the brother of the Lord (see Acts 12:17; 15:13; 21:18; Gal. 1:19).

Mothers and Sons

Walt Donner went to a party in Jerusalem where there were both Mediterranean-Judean and American friends of his. During the party he noticed that one of his Mediterranean-Judean friends was there without his wife, and he inquired if she were all right. The friend replied that his wife was very well but that she had remained home to make sure their oldest son studied hard for his exams. Walt felt that it was rather strange that a boy of thirteen should need his mother around to make him study, but Walt did not pursue the matter any further.

Why did the mother stay home to make her son study for exams?

Mary and Jesus, Mother and Son

Mediterranean-Judean mothers are very protective of their sons. Female adulthood is predicated on a good marriage with sons. Mothers need sons for their social standing. Furthermore, the family's honor rating and the parents' social security are all bound up with the son's successes. Sons are expected to live in or near the paternal house for the rest of their lives. Mediterranean mothers have developed a very protective role when dealing with their sons. That the mother in this episode stayed home with her son is but one illustration of the nature of her protective, nurturing role.

Even in biblical times, mothers were in charge of their sons until those sons moved into the world of men. Mary duly inquires of the early adolescent Jesus as to what he was up to on their pilgrimage to Jerusalem (Luke 2:48), indicating that Jesus had not yet fully passed into the world of males. The oldest son—"the only one in the sight of [his] mother" (Prov. 4:3)—was frequently the favorite. While in the women's sphere, mothers taught their sons traditional wisdom (e.g., Proverbs 31 contains "the words of Lemuel, king of Massa, which his mother taught him"—a son she received because of her vows, Prov. 31:2).

The mother's task was to develop a wise son, for "a foolish son is a sorrow to his mother" (Prov. 10:1); "a foolish man despises his mother" (Prov. 15:20); a son "who does violence to his father and chases away his mother is a son who causes shame and brings reproach" (Prov. 19:26). And the normal way to inculcate wisdom was painful discipline: "The rod and reproof give wisdom, but a child left to himself brings shame to his mother" (Prov. 29:15).

Proverbs offers divine sanctions against recalcitrant sons:

If one curses his father or his mother,
>   his lamp will be put out in utter darkness (Prov. 20:20);

the eye that mocks a father
>   and scorns to obey a mother
will be picked out by the ravens of the valley
>   and eaten by the vultures (Prov. 30:17).

Deuteronomy goes farther, it seems, for it gives parents the right to decide on the capital punishment of a recalcitrant son:

If a man has a stubborn and rebellious son, who will not obey the voice of his father or the voice of his mother, and, though they chastise him, will not give heed to them, then his father and his mother shall take hold of him and bring him out to the elders of his city at the gate of the place where he lives, and they shall say to the elders of his city, "This our son is stubborn and rebellious, he will not obey our voice; he is a glutton and a drunkard." Then all the men of the city shall stone him to death with stones; so you shall purge the evil from your midst; and all Israel shall hear, and fear (Deut. 21:18–21).

What ultimately counts is the honor of the father and of the embedded mother, hence of the existing family. Therefore: "'Cursed be he who dishonors his father or his mother.' And all the people shall say, 'Amen'" (Deut. 27:16).

Again, Sirach articulates traditional values as espoused by the elite, with his focus on the father, in whom the mother is socially embedded:

For the Lord honored the father above the children,
>   and he confirmed the right of the mother over her sons.
Whoever honors his father atones for sins,
>   and whoever glorifies his mother is like one who lays up treasure.
Whoever honors his father will be gladdened by his own children,
>   and when he prays he will be heard.
Whoever glorifies his father will have long life,
>   and whoever obeys the Lord will refresh his mother;
>   he will serve his parents as his masters.
Honor your father by word and deed,
>   that a blessing from him may come upon you.
For a father's blessing strengthens the houses of the children,
>   but a mother's curse uproots their foundations.
Do not glorify yourself by dishonoring your father,
>   for your father's dishonor is no glory to you.
For a man's glory comes from honoring his father,
>   and it is a disgrace for children not to respect their mother.
O son, help your father in his old age,
>   and do not grieve him as long as he lives;
even if he is lacking in understanding, show forbearance;
>   in all your strength do not despise him.
For kindness to a father will not be forgotten,

and against your sins it will be credited to you;
  in the day of your affliction it will be remembered in your favor;
    as frost in fair weather, your sins will melt away.
Whoever forsakes his father is like a blasphemer,
  and whoever angers his mother is cursed by the Lord (Sir. 3:2–16).

Without a son a female simply has no opportunity for recognition as a full person. Hence mothers are truly bound to their sons, forming a sort of group-oriented, mutually embedded set. This relationship is not that of one individualistic person with another. However, the relationship of mother to son is most often one of deep attachment, the relationship closest to what a North American would call love. Thus Sirach notes:

Be like a father to orphans,
  and instead of a husband to their mother;
you will then be like a son of the Most High,
  and he will love you more than does your mother (Sir. 4:10).

One must honor one's father and mother. Honor means to demonstrate their inestimable worth by means of one's words and practical deeds, that is, physical and material support. Why? Because the son has an irreparable debt of gratitude, a debt of interpersonal obligation, to parents. This debt of interpersonal obligation is called *hesed* in Hebrew, *eleios* in Greek. The English version of these words is "loving-kindness" or "mercy" (see Windows 39–41). Why this debt?

With all your heart honor your father,
  and do not forget the birth pangs of your mother.
Remember that through your parents you were born;
  and what can you give back to them that equals their gift to you? (Sir. 7:27–28).

Motherly Competition

While sitting at a sidewalk cafe in Capernaum, having a small cup of wine, Zach Melish noticed two Mediterranean-Judean women talking rather loudly to each other. They were standing across the street from each other, each one in front of her house. Eventually the discussion turned to their children, and how well they were doing. Both the women were rapt in their discussion when the children, adult sons, came walking down the road, home from a trip to Caesarea Philippi. Both mothers immediately asked their sons how they got on. One of the women crowed to her neighbor, "My son is getting very close to the prophet, Jesus. How is your son doing?" The other woman replied that her son was in his inner circle.

Zach was pleased that both boys were doing so well with the prophet. Yet he was very surprised to find out later that the mother of the son who said he was getting along with the prophet, but was not in his inner circle, refused to cook supper for her son.

What does this episode indicate about the Mediterranean-Judean mother-son relationship?

Gospel Mothers

Mediterranean-Judean mothers take intense pride in the achievements of their sons. While most mothers in most cultures are proud of their sons, this pride is exceptionally strong in first-century Palestine. The pride is, in part, an indication of the close ties between mother and son since the son stays embedded in the mother for as long as she lives. In a very true sense, she finds wholeness and a full life in the exploits of her son(s). The achievements of the son are seen as a very direct reflection on the merits of the mother. In this instance, the son who was getting close to the prophet did not reflect as much of his mother's merits as the son in the inner circle. She was probably embarrassed (relatively) by this performance, and she vented her resentment by refusing to cook supper for the son.

This relationship of mother to sons is illustrated well in the following Gospel incident:

> Then the mother of the sons of Zebedee came up to him, with her sons, and kneeling before him she asked him for something. And he said to her, "What do you want?" She said to him, "Command that these two sons of mine may sit, one at your right hand and one at your left, in your kingdom." But Jesus answered,

"You do not know what you are asking. Are you able to drink the cup that I am to drink?" They said to him, "We are able." He said to them, "You will drink my cup, but to sit at my right hand and at my left is not mine to grant, but it is for those for whom it has been prepared by my Father." And when the ten heard it, they were indignant at the two brothers (Matt. 20:20–24).

In this passage, Zebedee's wife behaves like a proper Mediterranean mother. The ten other disciples become angry with the brothers, not with the mother although the mother was the one who was responsible for the interaction. But she is really only acting as a mother must. The sons should have protested in favor of in-group loyalty rather than acquiesce in their mother's claim for their superiority. Furthermore, were the mothers of the ten around, they would have jumped on their sons for letting the Zebedee brothers get into such a relationship of confidence with Jesus to enable their mother to push for her sons as she did.

This scenario is normal first-century Judean and Mediterranean behavior. It is so normal that it is not at issue here. Zebedee's wife is neither reproved nor commended.

SUMMARY WINDOW

We have seen that Mediterranean-Judean parents generally adopt a very protective attitude toward their children of all ages, especially their sons. Mother-son ties were quite strong in first-century Palestine as they are in the contemporary Mediterranean. Often they do not break down until the son emigrates or is forced away from his native village, and thereby becomes somewhat independent. Finally, males play a more public role in Mediterranean-Judean culture than females do. Males attempt to gain honor for the family on the outside; they represent the family and its interests on the outside. Females remain embedded in and circumscribed by males, have their honor preserved and protected by males, and control the family on the inside. From an American point of view, the role of the Mediterranean-Judean female is a rather subservient one. In addition, the gender role distinction is clearly defined and sharply maintained.

FOR FURTHER READING

Malina, Bruce J. "Mary—Woman of the Mediterranean: Mother and Son." *Biblical Theology Bulletin* 20 (1990): 54–64.

Malina, Bruce J., and Jerome H. Neyrey. "Honor and Shame in Luke-Acts: Pivotal Values of the Mediterranean World." In *The Social World of Luke-Acts: Models for Interpretation*, edited by Jerome H. Neyrey. Peabody, Mass.: Hendrickson, 1991, 25–65.

Malina, Bruce J., and Jerome H. Neyrey. "First-Century Personality: Dyadic, Not Individual." In *The Social World of Luke-Acts: Models for Interpretation*, edited by Jerome H. Neyrey. Peabody, Mass.: Hendrickson, 1991, 67–96.

V

OUT-GROUP

INTRODUCTORY WINDOW

This series of episodes focuses on the role of the out-group in Mediterranean-Judean culture. The out-group boundaries were drawn in such a way that everyone knew who belonged to the out-group. And everyone knew the behavior proper to treating out-group members as well as the manner in which out-groups operated. Distinctions drawn between Judeans or "Jews and Greeks," or between "Israel and the (other) nations" (= Gentiles) refer to in-group–out-group distinctions. The distinction underscores lack of universal principles in interpersonal behavior since out-group members are rarely considered truly human or worthy of the respect one would give in-group members. The pain, suffering, and death of an out-group person is not worthy of consideration or concern. Thus if one is perceived as an out-group person, she or he would be considered to belong to a virtually different species of human being and treated accordingly.

Since U.S. ethics tend to be universalistic, to be applied to all persons because they are persons, Americans readily blunder in this matter when thrust into the Mediterranean-Judean scene. What is most striking is the lack of concern, indifference, and often disdain regularly shown to out-group members.

Polite Indifference

While in Judea, Hank Jones was working at a Mediterranean-Judean company as a supervisor. The first day he came to the office, he greeted everyone and introduced himself to one and all. After that, when he arrived in the morning, he would just go to his office without speaking to anyone and proceed to set up his schedule. He soon found that the Mediterranean Judeans appeared to treat him very coldly. They were not hostile, just somewhat indifferent. He did not understand why.

Why were the Mediterranean Judeans indifferent to Hank?

MEANINGS IN WINDOW 33

Why Not Jesus of Capernaum?

Hank, in not showing continued, daily concern for his Mediterranean-Judean co-workers, did not make much of an attempt to become part of their in-group. You will remember that Mediterranean Judeans tend to be friendly and helpful to in-group members only. From a U.S. perspective, these people seem indifferent and even hostile to others. Since Hank made no effort to become friends with his Mediterranean-Judean co-workers, that is, he made no effort to join their in-group, the Mediterranean Judeans saw no reason to be friendly with him.

If a person makes no effort to become friends with his Mediterranean-Judean co-workers, fellow inhabitants, colleagues, and the like, that is, if one makes no effort to join their in-group, Mediterranean Judeans see no reason to be congenial and friendly. It is a sort of tit-for-tat relationship in which it is up to the out-group person to take the initiative.

Hence, if one should wish to start up a group of any sort, one must look to one's in-group for recruits or one must become an in-group member of some other group or groups to find recruits. For example, consider Paul's exclamation:

> For though I am free from all men, I have made myself a slave to all, that I might win the more. To the Jews I became as a Jew, in order to win Jews; to those under the law I became as one under the law—though not being myself under the law—that I might win those under the law. To those outside the law I became as one outside the law—not being without law toward God but under the law of Christ—that I might win those outside the law. To the weak I became weak, that I might win the weak. I have become all things to all men, that I might by all means save some. I do it all for the sake of the gospel, that I may share in its blessings (1 Cor. 9:19–23).

To North Americans, such behavior seems rooted in expediency and lack of principle. However for a Mediterranean, it is based on the in-group–out-group principle.

Then, too, why did Jesus of Nazareth move to Capernaum? Jesus' moving to Capernaum may have had to do with local hostility in Nazareth, the perception of limited good by the natives who believed Jesus was striving to rise above the rest of the village, and the like. But it may also have to do with the fact that there simply were not a sufficient quantity of persons in Nazareth for the task Jesus had in mind. The very move to a larger village meant becoming part of the in-group that the village was. Yet because ancient Mediterraneans (and their animals) were categorized in terms of their place of origin, persons always remembered that Jesus was from Nazareth, thus "Jesus of Nazareth," not "Jesus of Capernaum."

In the Gospel story, we find that Jesus' in-group standing led to quick response to his plea for faction formation from five locals, or at least locals with in-group connections. While the Synoptics do not mention it, John's tradition tells of Peter, Andrew, and Philip coming from Bethsaida (John 1:44; 12:21). Furthermore, since women marry out as a rule, we can conclude that Peter's wife's family also lived in Capernaum, hence the scene with Peter's mother-in-law (unless the woman was a widow). John and James ben Zebedee were from Capernaum as was the "toll collector" Matthew (Matt. 9:9; Mark 2:14; and Luke 5:27 who calls him Levi; Luke 5:29 notes this Levi has a house in Capernaum). While not all of the well-known "Twelve" may have been from Capernaum or tied to that town (for a listing, see Mark 3:16–19 and parallels in Matt. 10:2–4; Luke 6:14–16; Acts 1:13), yet all of them were Galileans, as distinct from Judeans and Pereans (Acts 1:11: "Men of Galilee"; see Acts 2:5; John 21:2 mentions Nathanael of Cana).

The shifting boundaries of the in-group can cover Jesus' family, with an internal ranking of its own (James, the brother of the Lord, seems to have ranked first as in Acts 12:17; 15:13; see Gal. 1:19); his village of origin, Nazareth; his adopted town, Capernaum; his faction; his region, Galilee; his ethnic group of belonging, the house of Israel (e.g., Matt. 10:5).

Outsiders Don't Count

Ken, in describing his first day in Jerusalem to his friend Alex, was very upset. He commented on how he had tried to take a bus downtown but had been pushed out of the way twice by crowds trying to get on. Later, he attempted to take a cab, but just as he was about to get in, a woman ran across the street and got in the back seat from the other side of the vehicle. Ken decided to walk to his destination. He found, however, that this could be frustrating and danger-ous as well, due to the fact that he found himself constantly being made to step in the street to get out of the way of other people. He summed it up by saying "the whole day was like a game of chicken."

Why did the Mediterranean Judeans seem to behave so discourteously?

MEANINGS IN WINDOW 34

The Trial of Jesus, an Out-Group Person

Ken was a stranger to everyone, and as a result they did not bother to be courte-ous to him. In first-century Palestine there were strong distinctions made between in-group and out-group members. In-group members are shown the greatest courtesies, but these courtesies are rarely, if ever, extended to nonmembers. Strangers cannot be regarded as members of the in-group. Only face-to-face groups where a person can express concern for others can become in-groups. Consequently, Ken, being a stranger to those he encountered, was not felt to be one of them. Furthermore, his style of dress and haircut would give him away as an out-group person unless he walked along with local friends.

These clearly drawn lines bring us back to the question of who is a neighbor, who belongs in the in-group? See the passages presented in Windows 18 and 19. They are worth rereading here, this time with emphasis on what happens to those in the out-group.

The way Jesus was treated by the Judean elites in Jerusalem (the so-called trial and Passion of Jesus in Mark 14–15 and parallels) can best be understood in terms of the in-group–out-group contrast. Jesus of Nazareth in Galilee was surely an out-group person in Jerusalem for at least two reasons: he was a Galilean and not a Judean, and he belonged to the ranks of the nonelite and not the elite of Jerusalem. The fact that he was treated so cruelly by U.S. standards simply underscores how out-group persons are regarded by various Mediter-ranean in-groups!

How to Keep Friends

While working at the army base in Jerusalem, Luther Lund was warned by a number of his friends about Mediterranean Judeans. The friends told him that after he got to know some of the Mediterranean Judeans well, they would ask him to buy things for them at the base's post exchange or store. If Luther refused, he was told that the Mediterranean Judeans would get angry and probably end their friendship with him.

Luther was prepared for the problem. When his Mediterranean-Judean friend Yehuda asked him to get some cigarettes for him, Luther replied, "I would like to very much, Yehuda. You know there is nothing that I wouldn't do for you if I could. However, they won't let me. They will punish me severely if they find out I am buying things on base to distribute on the outside, and you wouldn't want that, would you?" Luther found that Yehuda was still his friend. Luther's friendship with Yehuda was not ruptured, even though he did not get the cigarettes for him.

How would you account for the persistence of their friendship?

Jesus' Out-Group Relationships

Luther had, in effect, assured Yehuda that he (Luther) was aware of his obligations to him. Luther's friendship with Yehuda made him a member of Yehuda's in-group. Hence, he was required to go out of his way for Yehuda, and he could expect Yehuda to take risks on his behalf in return. While Luther could not fulfill Yehuda's request (which would have been a great risk), he was wise enough to explain why he could not. Luther's explanation constituted an assurance that he still wished to belong to Yehuda's in-group, and that he would fulfill his obligations when it became possible to do so.

Friendship puts friends in contact with the various in-groups to which the individual friends belonged before they struck up their friendship. Contacts among friends of friends of friends, etc., is what enlarges one's in-group network and facilitates problem-solving of all sorts. And of course, even new friends are expected to go out of their way to do favors for each other. A friend could always expect a return favor, even under difficult circumstances. If a friend cannot fulfill a request, he must explain why and thus assure the other that he still wishes to belong to the other's in-group, and that he will fulfill his obligations when it becomes possible to do so. Yet such explanations run a thin edge between assurance and rejection.

Luke describes Jesus' invitation to some would-be followers (for Matthew, they were already disciples, see Matt. 8:21–22), along with with Jesus' reply:

> To another he said, "Follow me." But he said, "Lord, let me first go and bury my father." But he said to him, "Leave the dead to bury their own dead; but as for you, go and proclaim the kingdom of God." Another said, "I will follow you, Lord; but let me first say farewell to those at my home." Jesus said to him, "No one who puts his hand to the plow and looks back is fit for the kingdom of God" (Luke 9:59–62).

However, the sequence—request to an in-group member, rejection by unwillingness to go out of one's way, followed by anger by the in-group member making the request—is clearest in the Lukan version of the parable of the Great Supper (Luke 14:15–24; Matt. 22:1–14 has an altered version, with in-group elites simply ignoring a king's invitation):

> But they all alike began to make excuses. The first said to him, "I have bought a field, and I must go out and see it; I pray you, have me excused." And another said, "I have bought five yoke of oxen, and I go to examine them; I pray you, have me excused." And another said, "I have married a wife, and therefore I cannot come." So the servant came and reported this to his master. Then the householder in anger said to his servant, "Go out quickly to the streets and lanes of the city, and bring in the poor and maimed and blind and lame" (Luke 14:18–21).

American Spoiled Children

A five-year-old American child came to first-century Palestine with his parents. He was to stay with his Mediterranean-Judean grandparents for a couple of days. The first morning he was there, his grandmother fixed him an egg and took it in to him.

The little boy refused the egg because he did not really care for eggs and was not hungry at the time. The grandmother repeatedly pleaded with the boy to eat the egg, but he refused. Finally, the little boy said, "If eating the egg is so important, why don't you eat it?" The grandmother sent the boy back to his mother, saying that he was an ungrateful, spoiled child.

What really bothered the grandmother so that she would send the child back to his mother?

MEANINGS IN WINDOW 36

God's (Free) Gifts Must Be Repaid

In first-century Palestine, it is impolite to refuse offers of food, regardless of who offers it and when. But this alone does not explain the scenario. The little boy failed to show proper appreciation for his grandmother's hospitality and concern. The egg was a symbol of the grandmother's concern, and the child rejected it. The rejection is what angered the grandmother. It would have been wiser for the boy to accept the egg, even though he had no intention of eating it. His failure to accept the egg was indeed an ungrateful act from the Mediterranean-Judean point of view. And parents should have taught their child to accept what is offered with proper respect and compliance. However, look at the other alternatives also.

A gift of any sort usually is a symbol of a person's concern. Rejection of the gift will most often anger the giver. It is always better to accept the gift, even with the intention of not keeping it, than to reject it. Failure to accept a gift is an ungrateful act from the Mediterranean-Judean point of view. On the other hand, a gift may be rejected to indicate deep displeasure with the giver:

> Though they fast, I will not hear their cry, and though they offer burnt offering and cereal offering, I will not accept them; but I will consume them by the sword, by famine, and by pestilence (Jer. 14:12).

> Oh, that there were one among you who would shut the doors, that you might not kindle fire upon my altar in vain! I have no pleasure in you, says the LORD of

hosts, and I will not accept an offering from your hand. For from the rising of the sun to its setting my name is great among the nations, and in every place incense is offered to my name, and a pure offering; for my name is great among the nations, says the LORD of hosts. But you profane it when you say that the LORD's table is polluted, and the food for it may be despised. "What a weariness this is," you say, and you sniff at me, says the LORD of hosts. You bring what has been taken by violence or is lame or sick, and this you bring as your offering! Shall I accept that from your hand? says the LORD (Mal. 1:10–13).

When you offer oblations to me, I will turn my face from you; for I have rejected your feast days, and new moons, and circumcisions of the flesh. I sent to you my servants the prophets, but you have taken and slain them and torn their bodies in pieces; their blood I will require of you, says the Lord (2 Esdras 1:31–32).

And a gift may be accepted but put to no use: "Working together with him, then, we entreat you not to accept the grace of God in vain" (2 Cor. 6:1).

Paul too believed that one must repay a gift. The ancient Mediterranean, like all peasant societies, was a limited-good society. In such a society, there are no surpluses; everything that exists is already distributed, like land itself. Thus any person who has more of anything must have deprived someone else. In such social settings, people are not expected to deprive themselves of anything. If they give a gift, they expect to be repaid at some later occasion. Hence every gift must be repaid in some way. For example, in Paul's quotation from Job 41:11: "Or who has given a gift to him that he might be repaid?" (Rom. 11:35), the obvious idea is that gifts eventually require repayment. And this is the traditional Mediterranean idea. This applies as well to God's "free" gift as well. Since everyone knows that gifts have to be repaid, any mention of God's free gift is an exhortation to Christians to pay their debt (note that the word translated "grace" refers to God's patronage or favors on behalf of Christians, a form of gift):

Under the test of this service, you will glorify God by your obedience in acknowledging the gospel of Christ, and by the generosity of your contribution for them and for all others; while they long for you and pray for you, because of the surpassing grace of God in you. Thanks be to God for his inexpressible gift! (2 Cor. 9:13–15).

For by grace you have been saved through faith; and this is not your own doing, it is the gift of God—not because of works, lest any man should boast (Eph. 2:8–9).

There is one body and one Spirit, just as you were called to the one hope that belongs to your call, one Lord, one faith, one baptism, one God and Father of us all, who is above all and through all and in all. But grace was given to each of us according to the measure of Christ's gift (Eph. 4:4–7).

As each has received a gift, employ it for one another, as good stewards of God's varied grace (1 Peter 4:10).

Family Dropout

Barry Schwartz, a second-generation American of Mediterranean-Judean parentage, returned to first-century Palestine for a three-month vacation. One of his distant relatives introduced him to this relative's niece. Barry knew that his relatives were interested in setting up a marriage, but Barry just was not interested.

Three weeks later, a messenger came from the girl's parents telling Barry that the girl would be in Jerusalem the following week with her parents. Barry knew that he should call his relatives and offer to arrange accommodations for their stay in Jerusalem or to have dinner with them. But since he was not interested in marriage with the girl, he decided to let the matter drop. He was very surprised when all of his relatives began to shun him.

Why did Barry's relatives begin to shun him?

Traditional Biblical Views on Friends and Enemies

Barry's relatives expected him to go out of his way to arrange to meet the girl and her parents. This expectation was rooted in Barry's in-group membership. His failure to make the effort to visit with them in Jerusalem angered his relatives and caused them to shun him. By failing to make the necessary effort, Barry was, in effect, alienating himself from his in-group and placing himself in the out-group. Consequently, he was treated coldly, that is in a manner customarily accorded to out-group members.

By failing to go out of their way to do what is necessary even if cumbersome, persons in effect alienate themselves from their in-group and place themselves in the out-group. They will henceforth be treated as out-group persons. Thus it is common to exhort people to go out of their way for their friends, for in-group friends provide the best social security in this sort of social system. Says Sirach: "In great and small matters do not act amiss, and do not become an enemy instead of a friend" (Sir. 5:15). And more specifically: "Lose your silver for the sake of a brother or a friend, and do not let it rust under a stone and be lost" (Sir. 29:10). More fully, we find:

> A friend will not be known in prosperity,
> nor will an enemy be hidden in adversity.

97

A man's enemies are grieved when he prospers,
    and in his adversity even his friend will separate from him.
Never trust your enemy,
    for like the rusting of copper, so is his wickedness.
Even if he humbles himself and goes about cringing,
    watch yourself, and be on your guard against him;
and you will be to him like one who has polished a mirror,
    and you will know that it was not hopelessly tarnished.
Do not put him next to you,
    lest he overthrow you and take your place;
do not have him sit at your right,
    lest he try to take your seat of honor,
and at last you will realize the truth of my words,
    and be stung by what I have said (Sir. 12:8–12).

Even after a person dies, his favors to his friends continue by means of his sons. For a good son, after his father dies, will be "an avenger against his enemies, and one to repay the kindness of his friends" (Sir. 30:6).

Proverbs has somewhat similar perspectives: "Your friend, and your father's friend, do not forsake; and do not go to your brother's house in the day of your calamity. Better is a neighbor who is near than a brother who is far away" (Prov. 27:10). And Sirach muses:

Some companions rejoice in the happiness of a friend,
    but in time of trouble are against him.
Some companions help a friend for their stomachs' sake,
    and in the face of battle take up the shield.
Do not forget a friend in your heart,
    and be not unmindful of him in your wealth (Sir. 37:4–6).

So much for Sirach, but these ideas are simply part of the cultural heritage. Job would have one always ready to do favors for friends: "He who withholds kindness from a friend forsakes the fear of the Almighty" (6:14). Proverbs notes that it is especially in difficult times that these favors are to be given: "A friend loves at all times, and a brother is born for adversity" (Prov. 17:17).

Rude Americans

Harvey Pace had been in first-century Palestine for a couple of years. He had become good friends with quite a few Mediterranean Judeans. One fellow, Benjamin ben Lev, was especially close, and they did lots of things together. One afternoon late in July, Harvey heard that one of his college buddies, Lenny, would be in Jerusalem the following week.

Lenny and Harvey had a grand reunion. Lenny wished to see the sights, and Harvey was quite willing to show him around. But Harvey wanted Benjamin to meet Lenny, so he asked Benjamin to come along with them.

In the course of their touring, Lenny and Harvey joked a lot with each other in the very sarcastic and critical manner that is often typical of American humor. Later in the evening it was apparent that Benjamin was not having a good time. When Lenny excused himself for a moment, Harvey asked Benjamin what was the matter. Benjamin replied that he was sorry that Lenny and Harvey were not getting along so well after all these years.

Why did Benjamin feel that Lenny and Harvey were not getting along?

MEANINGS IN WINDOW 38

Jesus' Public Put-downs

The sarcastic joking that took place between Lenny and Harvey made Benjamin feel ill at ease and, eventually, depressed. The way Lenny and Harvey carried on was perceived, in terms of first-century Palestinian standards, to mean that the two people were not getting along. It is behavior that a Mediterranean Judean would expect to take place between competitors, challengers, or out-group members. Friends in first-century Palestine do not behave in this fashion. Benjamin began to feel the way he did because Lenny and Harvey were not as affectionate toward each other as Mediterranean Judeans would be in a similar situation.

Sarcastic remarks are directed to out-group persons, to enemies. For example, whenever Jesus' enemies attack or attempt to publicly humiliate him, he responds quite sarcastically, usually with an insulting counterquestion. For example, consider how many times he asks Torah experts: "Have you not read . . . ?" Such words directed to persons who devote their lives to reading the Torah are extremely sarcastic:

> And as for the dead being raised, have you not read in the book of Moses, in the passage about the bush, how God said to him, "I am the God of Abraham, and the God of Isaac, and the God of Jacob?" (Mark 12:26; par. Matt. 22:31–32).

99

He said to them, "Have you not read what David did, when he was hungry, and those who were with him?" (Matt. 12:3; par. Luke 6:3).

Or have you not read in the law how on the sabbath the priests in the temple profane the sabbath, and are guiltless? (Matt. 12:5).

He answered, "Have you not read that he who made them from the beginning made them male and female?" (Matt. 19:4).

And as for the resurrection of the dead, have you not read what was said to you by God? (Matt. 22:31).

Have you not read this scripture:
"The very stone which the builders rejected
has become the head of the corner" (Mark 12:10).

Furthermore, when questions of Torah law (*halakah*) are put in the form of an obviously apparent answer, that is a similarly sarcastic ploy:

And he said to them, "Is it lawful on the sabbath to do good or to do harm, to save life or to kill?" But they were silent (Mark 3:4; par. Luke 6:9).

And Jesus spoke to the lawyers and Pharisees, saying, "Is it lawful to heal on the sabbath, or not?" (Luke 14:3).

And Luke describes Paul as employing similar sarcasm (although Paul's letters witness his own sarcastic ability):

But when they had tied him up with the thongs, Paul said to the centurion who was standing by, "Is it lawful for you to scourge a man who is a Roman citizen, and uncondemned?" (Acts 22:25).

SUMMARY WINDOW

In the Mediterranean, a person can know that he is "out-group" if he is treated in a cold and apparently inconsiderate way. Out-group members can expect no favors, no help involving inconvenience of the helper—instead they should anticipate the reverse. A person becomes out-group if he fails to show concern for another person or if he fails to reciprocate a friendly gesture, and so on. It should be noted that "dual status" is most common: a person usually belongs to several in-groups and several out-groups.

FOR FURTHER READING

Malina, Bruce J. *The New Testament World: Insights from Cultural Anthropology*, 2d ed. Louisville, Ky.: Westminster/John Knox Press, 1993.

Neyrey, Jerome H. "Unclean, Common, Polluted, and Taboo: A Short Reading Guide." *Forum* 4/4 (1988): 72–82.

Pilch, John J. "Lying and Deceit in the Letters to the Seven Churches: Perspectives from Cultural Anthropology." *Biblical Theology Bulletin* 22 (1992): 126–135.

VI

LOVING-KINDNESS

INTRODUCTORY WINDOW

In the Mediterranean world, persons feel obliged to be willing to go out of their way, to take risks, to make allowances for the sake of fellow in-group members, ranging from parents to friends and guests. In-group members sense that they owe each other a sort of debt of gratitude. And their willingness to go out of their way often involves considerable personal effort and cost on behalf of others. In English versions of the Old Testament, this specific obligation is often translated "loving-kindness" (Hebrew *hesed*). In the New Testament it is called "mercy" or "love" (Greek *eleos* or *agape*).

Perhaps the best short translation of this value is "willingness to pay one's debt of interpersonal obligation." (In modern Greek, a person who embodies this value is called *philotimos*). Since the obligation looks to in-group members, it clearly is closely related to the in-group–out-group distinction. In the following Windows the value is considered as it applies to family members, friends, hosts, and guests.

A Case of Bad Social Credit

Some American industrialists decided to set up a joint economic venture with a local Mediterranean-Judean company that would be run by both Mediterranean-Judean and American personnel. One of the first problems encountered was how to choose the personnel. The Americans had a list of Mediterranean-Judean men who had, through work and ability, left their past behind and become relatively successful. In U.S. estimation, these men would make very good managers for the new enterprise. However, whenever the men on this list were mentioned to local contacts, the Mediterranean Judeans considered these recommendations really off the mark. They said that these were really bad choices, that many of these men were really ungrateful persons. The Americans did not understand what was wrong with the men on their list.

What was wrong with the successful Mediterranean-Judean men?

MEANINGS IN WINDOW 39

Loving-Kindness Means Debt of Gratitude

The men on the list were remiss in paying their interpersonal debt of gratitude; they had violated the ideal of "loving-kindness." "Loving-kindness" requires a person to be loyal to in-group members regardless of the circumstances in which one might find oneself. In their pursuit of success, the men on the American list had virtually cut off contact with their in-groups ("they left their past behind . . ."). This is unforgivable disloyalty. And it is their disloyalty that accounts for the negative recommendations on the part of local Mediterranean Judeans.

Strong perception and awareness of an in-group–out-group contrast can be readily detected in all Mediterranean explanations of interpersonal relations. The in-group–out-group contrast is a basic theme, replicated in friend-enemy contrast. Reality in Mediterranean societies is always impregnated with social considerations, whereas in the United States, the assessment of situations is focused on the individual. Mediterraneans define the universe in terms of the triumphs of the in-group over the out-group, of family/friends/ethnic group over enemies/outsiders/the rest of humankind. Mediterranean social behavior is strongly dependent on whether "the other person" is a member of one's in-group or not. Key values are just and good depending on the way in which they are prismed through in-group–out-group and according to the relevance they have with regard to this fundamental contrast. All relations, whether with authority figures, patrons, employers, merchants, even with persons with whom one is in conflict, are perceived and nuanced in terms of the in-group–out-group contrast.

"Loving-kindness," "mercy," or "love" (depending on one's Bible translation), for example, requires a person to be loyal to in-group members. As indicated in the scenario, upon analysis we find that successful men have virtually cut off contact with their in-groups. Normally the in-group would make constant demands on the time and resources of a more successful relative or friend. Hence to curtail opportunities for the in-group to make such demands, successful men cut off contact with their in-groups. The result of such a strategy leaves their honor in doubt. Hence successful persons are usually rated as disloyal, for if they remained loyal to their in-group of origin, they would not have stepped out of the dead-level equality of that in-group and surely would never have become successful, presumably at the cost of one's in-group members. This attitude is perfectly summed up in the line from 2 Maccabees: "success at the cost of one's kindred is the greatest misfortune" (2 Macc. 5:6). Hence successful persons can only be given negative recommendations from their original in-group members.

The successful Jesus "of Nazareth," whose fame spread after he took up residence in Capernaum, is an example of this process. All the Synoptics have an account of Jesus breaking with his original in-group, his family. Mark's version is the strongest, since after a particularly successful tour, his family comes looking for him (and worrying about their in-group honor) because people are saying negative things about Jesus:

> Then he went home [to Capernaum, see Mark 2:1]; and the crowd came together again, so that they could not even eat. And when his family heard it, they went out to seize him, for people were saying, "He is beside himself." And the scribes who came down from Jerusalem said, "He is possessed by Beelzebul, and by the prince of demons he casts out the demons" (Mark 3:19–22).

After a discussion between Jesus and these Jerusalem scribes, a primary confrontational out-group in Mark, we are told:

> And his mother and his brothers came; and standing outside they sent to him and called him. And a crowd was sitting about him; and they said to him, "Your mother and your brothers are outside, asking for you." And he replied, "Who are my mother and my brothers?" And looking around on those who sat about him, he said, "Here are my mother and my brothers! Whoever does the will of God is my brother, and sister, and mother" (Mark 3:31–35).

Unlike Mark, Matthew and Luke say nothing about the motive for the presence of Jesus' family, but both note Jesus' distancing himself from his family (and like Mark, both Matthew and Luke note the absence of the family at Jesus' death):

While he was still speaking to the people, behold, his mother and his brothers stood outside, asking to speak to him. But he replied to the man who told him, "Who is my mother, and who are my brothers?" And stretching out his hand toward his disciples, he said, "Here are my mother and my brothers! For whoever does the will of my Father in heaven is my brother, and sister, and mother" (Matt. 12:46–50).

Then his mother and his brothers came to him, but they could not reach him for the crowd. And he was told, "Your mother and your brothers are standing outside, desiring to see you." But he said to them, "My mother and my brothers are those who hear the word of God and do it" (Luke 8:19–21).

On the other hand, in defense of the successful person, members of subsequent in-groups can always point up the dishonorable nature of the original in-group. Thus while Luke absolves the family of Jesus, noting their significant presence in Jerusalem after the Resurrection (Acts 1:14), he explains Jesus' move from the original Nazareth in-group—that is, Jesus' family and relatives—as motivated by active hostility on the part of the wider in-group, the villagers of Nazareth:

And he came to Nazareth, where he had been brought up; and he went to the synagogue, as his custom was, on the sabbath day. And he stood up to read, and there was given to him the book of the prophet Isaiah. . . . And all spoke well of him, and wondered at the gracious words which proceeded out of his mouth; and they said, "Is not this Joseph's son?" And he said to them, "Doubtless you will quote to me this proverb, 'Physician, heal yourself; what we have heard you did at Capernaum, do here also in your own country.'" And he said, "Truly, I say to you, no prophet is acceptable in his own country. But in truth, I tell you, there were many widows in Israel in the days of Elijah, when the heaven was shut up three years and six months, when there came a great famine over all the land; and Elijah was sent to none of them but only to Zarephath, in the land of Sidon, to a woman who was a widow. And there were many lepers in Israel in the time of the prophet Elisha; and none of them was cleansed, but only Naaman the Syrian." When they heard this, all in the synagogue were filled with wrath. And they rose up and put him out of the city, and led him to the brow of the hill on which their city was built, that they might throw him down headlong. But passing through the midst of them he went away.
And he went down to Capernaum, a city of Galilee (Luke 4:16–17, 22–31).

Mark indicates that he believed Jesus was from Nazareth; he has no mention of birth in Bethlehem. John, for his part, believed Jesus' origin was from God (John 1:1–14) and ignores any other geographical origin:

When they heard these words, some of the people said, "This is really the prophet." Others said, "This is the Christ." But some said, "Is the Christ to come from Galilee? Has not the scripture said that the Christ is descended from David, and comes from Bethlehem, the village where David was?" So there was a division among the people over him. Some of them wanted to arrest him, but no one laid hands on him (John 7:40–44).

Matthew and Luke, in turn, believe Jesus was born in Bethlehem (Matt. 2:1; Luke 2:4). Yet they do not call him Jesus "of Bethlehem" perhaps because the Bethlehem birth was deduced to have been "irregular."

Yet in the whole Gospel tradition, Jesus' primary in-group came from Nazareth. Even John mentions "Jesus of Nazareth, the son of Joseph" in a context where we learn of the stereotypical assessment of Nazareth, when Nathanael said to him, "Can anything good come out of Nazareth?" (John 1:45–46).

The Obligated, Unhappy Brother

Matt Landaw had spent a lot of time in one of the Mediterranean-Judean villages, studying local agricultural techniques. After a short time he had come to know everyone in the village and would meet the men at the local cafe in the evening. One of the young Mediterranean-Judean men that came there every night was single and highly praised by all the other men because he was working very hard to build up his sister's dowry (she was still unmarried). Everyone commented on what a fine thing he was doing, yet whenever this young man would come to the cafe he would always remind everyone what he was doing and say things like, "Isn't it sad that I should have to remain single when everyone else can get married." Matt couldn't understand why everyone continued to be sympathetic.

Why were the other men so sympathetic?

MEANINGS IN WINDOW 40

Redeemers Pay Debts of Gratitude

The young man was obliged to do something that he didn't particularly care to do (build up his sister's dowry). Building up his sister's dowry was an in-group obligation deriving from the debt of interpersonal obligation ("loving-kindness") that he owed his family. And the young man did not care for this obligation. The other men realized that he had to do this, even though he didn't want to. Hence the sympathy.

In-group obligations have little to do with wanting or not wanting to fulfill them. Fulfilling them is a matter of loyalty and group solidarity, even fulfilling them begrudgingly. Other people in the society are well aware of the types of in-group obligations persons have. By applauding persons who fulfill their obligations, even with resentment, the one fulfilling the obligation receives a grant of honor, at times coupled with sympathy and understanding.

The general category of in-group obligations is in fact "debts of interpersonal obligation." Now such in-group obligations arise from implicit in-group "contracts" by means of which persons are seen to be bound to each other, for example, by birth, by marriage, by having one's life saved by another. The interpersonal obligations that arise from such contracts are a form of generalized reciprocity. Such generalized reciprocity is a back-and-forth interaction among unequals in which the initiating or preceding parties can never really be paid back. For example, who can pay back a parent for life, a first-born child for opening the womb and allowing the other children to be born, a sibling for the benefits of growing up together, a wife for the children she bears, a husband for supporting wife and children, or God for initiating relationships with human beings.

Thus children, so long as they live, have such a debt of interpersonal obligation toward their parents. Specifically the debt is to "honor your father and mother," that is, to give physical support and respect, to speak well of, and to maintain the parents' honor by one's conduct. Siblings (with precedence going to the first-born male) and spouses (with precedence going to the husband) have such debts toward each other, as do in-group friends and village mates and persons who save another.

In this context, a redeemer (Hebrew, *go'el*; see Window 2) is a son or other male relative who attempts to get satisfaction for dishonor done to the family. The role of redeemer functions in terms of this debt. The debt also motivates persons to buy back enslaved relatives, reacquire lost family lands, or defend the honor of an in-group superior, usually a patron, whether king, noble, landowner, or the like.

The title "redeemer" attributed to Jesus indicates that some considered his career in terms of in-group obligations. The Gospel tradition that underscores the need for Jesus to go up to Jerusalem and to be killed there points in the same direction—Jesus as one who pays his interpersonal obligations on behalf of his in-group.

The Friend Who Meant Well

Jeff Uhlman constantly went to the same restaurant while he was in Capernaum. Because of this, he got to know the management well. In particular he had one waiter who served him all the time. This waiter would serve him quickly and be very polite with helpful suggestions as well.

One evening Jeff brought two of his American friends along for dinner. After the meal, there was the usual American argument over the bill. The waiter, upon seeing this, gave the bill immediately to Jeff, his usual customer. One of the other Americans laughed at Jeff and said, "With friends like that, who needs enemies?"

Why did the waiter give Jeff the check?

Ancient Service and Sales

The waiter thought he was doing Jeff a favor by siding with him in the argument. Because Jeff had eaten at the restaurant often and had come to know that particular waiter quite well, the waiter came to consider Jeff as a member of his in-group. In Judea, it is expected that one always sides with a member of the in-group during an argument—whether that person is correct or not. As a result, upon seeing Jeff arguing with two others, the waiter immediately sided with Jeff and gave him the check. Likewise the concept of honor—of being a good host—is very important in Judea. It is expected that one will always be honorable. Thus, the waiter felt that by giving Jeff the check, he was properly paying a debt of gratitude by helping Jeff to be honorable.

In the ancient Mediterranean, the activity of buying and selling was always tilted in favor of the seller. In other words, it was always a seller's market. The buyer simply had to beware. And the buyer inevitably had to cover for any seller error, for example, overcharge, faulty merchandise, insufficient amount of goods, and the like. The interaction was stacked so much in favor of the seller that it was assumed a person need not be ashamed "of profit from dealing with merchants" (Sir. 42:5). Buying and selling was antagonistic, a haggling affair. Sirach warned: "A merchant can hardly keep from wrongdoing, and a tradesman will not be declared innocent of sin" (26:29). For him it was axiomatic that "As a stake is driven firmly into a fissure between stones, so sin is wedged in between selling and buying" (27:2). The only way to overcome being taken advantage of was to become part of the seller's in-group. And this usually happened when a person frequented the same seller often.

Certain arrangements are made, often implicitly, as the buyer comes to know a particular merchant quite well, and the merchant comes to consider the regular buyer as a member of his in-group. The buyer becomes a "client" entitled to "favors."

In Judea, as in the Mediterranean in general, it is expected that one shows favor to in-group members and always sides with them during an argument—whether that member is correct or not. This is important to keep in mind since all the ancient Christian writings that have come down to us are in-group writings preserved by in-group members for the in-group. Those who preserved those writings and those who heard them read always sided with the position taken in them. Of course, the same is true of other writings preserved by other in-groups.

SUMMARY WINDOW

Loving-kindness ("mercy," "love") was the central concept in the preceding series. Roughly speaking, loving-kindness implies loyalty to and solidarity with in-group members rooted in a debt of gratitude to all those persons. It is a sort of obligatory willingness to yield to the welfare needs of these significant others. A person is willing to go out of one's way, expend effort, take risks, make allowances for friends or other members of the family. For example, a Mediterranean Judean is expected to put up with even the most unpleasant situations on behalf of family and friends (like housing them, if necessary). Finally, loving-kindness requires that one be ready to entertain in-group members at any time.

FOR FURTHER READING

Malina, Bruce J. "Patron and Client: The Analogy Behind Synoptic Theology." *Forum* 4/1 (1988): 1–32.
———. "Dealing with Biblical (Mediterranean) Characters: A Guide for U.S. Consumers." *Biblical Theology Bulletin* 19 (1989): 127–141.

VII

COMMON VALUES

INTRODUCTORY WINDOW

In the first-century Mediterranean, the kinship group was the producing unit as well as the consuming unit. The societies of the time, in spite of their variations, were all peasant societies with a slave component. "Peasant society" refers to a society focused on a central place, the preindustrial city, which served as administrative political center and invariably housed some central temple(s) under the aegis of those in power.

The purpose of working in such societies was not to get ahead. Work was meant to maintain a person and his family within one's inherited status. Jobs were performed in terms of honor and shame, hence with great emphasis upon not making mistakes that others might come to know. Job security depended on one's patron, if one could find a person to act as patron. Criticism of one's work was always personal, reflecting the sort of human being one was judged to be. And hiring practices followed kinship lines (as did religious practices as well).

Never Make a Mistake

An American, Kyle McCusker, was discussing his two-year stay in Judea with a number of U.S. friends. They got around to the topic of work and work relations. Kyle related some of his experiences. He summed up his experience by saying that he had never found a Mediterranean Judean who had made a mistake. Most of the people who had been in Judea laughed at Kyle's remark. But the rest of the group seemed puzzled. They failed to see the humor in the remark so they asked Kyle to explain what he meant by saying he had never found a local person who made a mistake.

What was Kyle's explanation?

Decisions Are to Be Avoided

Mediterranean Judeans and Americans are evaluated by superiors and rewarded by the institutions for which they work in quite different ways. In Judea, workers are generally rewarded (promoted) if they have reached a certain age, been loyal to the organization, and made no mistakes during their careers. Americans are rewarded as much for their accomplishments as for their lack of mistakes. The point is that it is essential for Mediterranean Judeans to avoid mistakes (or at least avoid having them exposed) if they are to be promoted. Furthermore, mistakes frequently result in dishonor (blushing, called "blackening of the face") or a "loss of face." Consequently, Mediterranean-Judean workers are very reluctant to admit any errors that they may have made because it reflects on both them and their in-group.

Then too, the concept of "mistake" is alien to Mediterranean-Judean culture. This concept implies weaknesses or flaws, and Mediterranean Judeans tend to regard such things as the outcome of fate (Greek, *moira*; Latin, *fortuna*) or God's providence—rather than being the result of their own actions. Now while this explanation may be applicable to the hindsight assessment of a major period of one's life or one's life in general, it does not pertain to individual pieces of behavior. Persons are believed responsible for their actions—yet there is the overall control by fate or providence as well, to be seen in hindsight.

Furthermore, elites on a career ladder (which the Romans called a *cursus honorum*, a sequence of honors), or people in elite roles attain their social positions essentially through birth (although at times it might be a combination of proper birth and patronage). Promotion invariably follows on the basis of age, loyalty, and, as previously noted, a lack of significant mistakes during one's career. Thus the proper course of behavior for elites is to avoid initiative and not permit any sort of deviation from the status quo unless a ready scapegoat is available.

In the Gospel story, Pilate is a good example of this elite attitude. He makes no decision about Jesus' death but rather goes along with the wishes of Judean elites and the crowd. In effect the Judean elites and the crowd make the decision. If an error is committed, it is their fault. Pilate makes no decision. He does not command the Judean elites to back off, nor does he command Jesus to be killed. In effect, he does nothing wrong but merely permits events to happen:

> Now at the feast the governor was accustomed to release for the crowd any one prisoner whom they wanted. And they had then a notorious prisoner, called Barabbas. So when they had gathered, Pilate said to them, "Whom do you want me to release for you, Barabbas or Jesus who is called Christ?" For he knew that it was out of envy that they had delivered him up. Besides, while he was sitting on the judgment seat, his wife sent word to him, "Have nothing to do with that righteous man, for I have suffered much over him today in a dream." Now the chief priests and the elders persuaded the people to ask for Barabbas and destroy Jesus. The governor again said to them, "Which of the two do you want me to release for you?" And they said, "Barabbas." Pilate said to them, "Then what shall I do with Jesus who is called Christ?" They all said, "Let him be crucified." And he said, "Why, what evil has he done?" But they shouted all the more, "Let him be crucified."
>
> So when Pilate saw that he was gaining nothing, but rather that a riot was beginning, he took water and washed his hands before the crowd, saying, "I am innocent of this man's blood; see to it yourselves." And all the people answered, "His blood be on us and on our children!" Then he released for them Barabbas, and having scourged Jesus, delivered him to be crucified (Matt. 27:15–26; see also Mark 15:6–16 and Luke 23:13–25).

In this perspective, should events occur to the detriment of an elite person like Pilate, one would blame it on fate or fortune or providence, never on one's choices since no choices were really made (except the choice to do nothing, the proper choice since one is not responsible for doing nothing!). Thus in Acts, Pilate is remembered as follows:

> The God of Abraham and of Isaac and of Jacob, the God of our fathers, glorified his servant Jesus, whom you delivered up and denied in the presence of Pilate, when he had decided to release him. But you denied the Holy and Righteous One, and asked for a murderer to be granted to you, and killed the Author of life, whom God raised from the dead. To this we are witnesses (Acts 3:13–15).

> For truly in this city there were gathered together against thy holy servant Jesus, whom thou didst anoint, both Herod and Pontius Pilate, with the Gentiles and the peoples of Israel, to do whatever thy hand and thy plan had predestined to take place (Acts 4:27–28).

115

For those who live in Jerusalem and their rulers, because they did not recognize him nor understand the utterances of the prophets which are read every sabbath, fulfilled these by condemning him. Though they could charge him with nothing deserving death, yet they asked Pilate to have him killed. And when they had fulfilled all that was written of him, they took him down from the tree, and laid him in a tomb (Acts 13:27–29).

Never Admit Ignorance

Jerry Clark was having difficulty with the American automobile that he had brought to Judea with him. He looked up the name of an automobile mechanic in the phone book and drove his car over to the shop.

When he arrived, Jerry asked the mechanic if he had ever worked on this type of car before. The Mediterranean Judean quickly replied, "Yes, of course." Jerry was satisfied and started to leave. When he was almost out of the shop, however, he turned to watch the mechanic begin his work. He was astonished by what he saw. It took the mechanic several minutes to figure out how to raise the hood.

How can the mechanic's statement be explained?

MEANINGS IN WINDOW 43

Unfamiliarity Is Not to Be Admitted

Although the mechanic had never worked on this type of car, he would not admit it. Mediterranean Judeans do not like to admit they are unable to perform functions relating to their jobs or any other social roles, with the obligations and rights bound up with them. To admit inability would be an indication that they are not only incapable workers, but also bad spouses, fathers, and the like. Further, to be unable to fulfill one's social role indicates one is expendable, dismissible, not necessary within the in-group that work groups form. In other words, since Mediterranean Judeans do not separate occupation and personal life, a person's admission that he was unfamiliar with some role-related problem would be a challenge to his own self-worth, to his core sense of honor.

In this regard, note that the Gospel story preserves a tradition in which Jesus, Peter, James, and John come down the mountain after the Transfiguration to join the rest of the disciples, who presumably were healing people. Mark describes the scene as follows:

> And when they came to the disciples, they saw a great crowd about them, and scribes arguing with them. And immediately all the crowd, when they saw him, were greatly amazed, and ran up to him and greeted him. And he asked them, "What are you discussing with them?" And one of the crowd answered him, "Teacher, I brought my son to you, for he has a dumb spirit; and wherever it seizes him, it dashes him down; and he foams and grinds his teeth and becomes rigid; and I asked your disciples to cast it out, and they were not able" (Mark 9:14–18).

The point is the disciples do not say anything in public about their inability to heal; after all they are disciples, therefore they can heal. The questioning happens in private, where honor is safeguarded (the Markan literary pattern of public discussion, private explanation, serves a similar end—the private explanation preserves the disciples' honor as well as conceals information from the public, especially from opponents):

> And when he had entered the house, his disciples asked him privately, "Why could we not cast it out?" And he said to them, "This kind cannot be driven out by anything but prayer" (Mark 9:28–29).

This relationship between social role and presumed ability to handle the role is not unlike the U.S. presupposition that women who give birth to children are automatically capable of being "good" mothers. In no other area of life do Americans identify social role and capability without question as they do in mothering. And even U.S. courts generally award children to mothers on the presumption that mothers "naturally" do better at child rearing! This presumption is part of the inherited wisdom that equates social role and the ability to perform the role.

The proverbial put-down, "Physician, heal yourself" (Luke 4:23), relates to this Mediterranean presupposition. Those with the social role of physicians were presumed to be healthy and to be able to stay healthy. Moreover, they should be able to heal whomever they treat. In fact, physicians would never treat a person they could not heal or who might die, lest they be dishonored (or charged with the death of their patient). Similarly in the Gospels, the fact that disciples call Jesus "Messiah" would lead one to expect Jesus to do messianic things. Presumably, one of these messianic things is the ability to call upon God for help. Hence the reaction at the crucifixion:

> And those who passed by derided him, wagging their heads and saying, "You who would destroy the temple and build it in three days, save yourself! If you are the Son of God, come down from the cross." So also the chief priests, with the scribes and elders, mocked him, saying, "He saved others; he cannot save himself. He is the King of Israel; let him come down now from the cross, and we will believe in him. He trusts in God; let God deliver him now, if he desires him; for he said, 'I am the Son of God.'" And the robbers who were crucified with him also reviled him in the same way (Matt. 27:39–44; see also Mark 15:29–32 and Luke 23:35–39).

That nothing happens belies the claimant's ascribed role and shames him in public —the whole point of the crucifixion from the viewpoint of Jesus' enemies.

Consider the interaction in the following scenario, in which Jesus, the non-fisherman, tells fishermen their business:

> And he saw two boats by the lake; but the fishermen had gone out of them and were washing their nets. . . . And when he had ceased speaking, he said to Simon,

"Put out into the deep and let down your nets for a catch." And Simon answered, "Master, we toiled all night and took nothing! But at your word I will let down the nets." And when they had done this, they enclosed a great shoal of fish; and as their nets were breaking, they beckoned to their partners in the other boat to come and help them. And they came and filled both the boats, so that they began to sink. But when Simon Peter saw it, he fell down at Jesus' knees, saying "Depart from me, for I am a sinful man, O Lord." For he was astonished, and all that were with him, at the catch of fish which they had taken; and so also were James and John, sons of Zebedee, who were partners with Simon. And Jesus said to Simon, "Do not be afraid; henceforth you will be catching men." And when they had brought their boats to land, they left everything and followed him (Luke 5:2, 4–11).

When the episode ends, one would expect to hear about how when the boats docked, the fishermen sold the fish and thus all earned a great amount of money. But instead, when the boats docked, Simon, James, and John leave everything to follow Jesus. How would the episode prepare the reader for such a conclusion? Does the proof of Jesus' ability to outdo professional fishermen earn admiration and respect along with willingness to cooperate in Jesus' project?

Schedules Are Not Important

An American executive, Kent Watson, called in one of his Mediterranean-Judean subordinates to ask him to prepare a report. He asked the employee to estimate how much time he thought it would take to complete the report, and the Mediterranean Judean estimated about ten days. Kent told him that even fifteen days would be fine.

On the afternoon of the fifteenth day, Kent called his subordinate in and asked for the report. The Mediterranean Judean reassured him that he would have it in the morning. Kent got upset and said, "But, Menachem, the report was due today."

Menachem replied, "I know, but it's almost closing time, and it will be in tomorrow first thing in the morning."

Kent told Menachem that having the report ready on time was a matter of principle. But Menachem exploded and told Kent that he had worked nights and had given up his recreation and had even worked on the Sabbath as well.

With this, Kent realized that the problem was due to a lack of planning. He told Menachem that he should not have worked at home but rather that he should have planned his time better and perhaps organized his work more efficiently.

From that day on, however, it was obvious to Kent that Menachem was resentful, obstinate, and very reluctant to continue his work. How can we best explain Menachem's behavior?

MEANINGS IN WINDOW 44

The Inefficiency of Others Is to Be Overlooked

Mediterranean Judeans do not believe it is important to keep to a schedule as do Americans. Menachem felt that he was personally attacked when Kent Watson criticized him for tardiness. Being on time was simply not a paramount value. Further, since Menachem had done almost all of the job, he felt that Watson should have complimented him for the part of the task already completed. That is, Mediterranean Judeans feel that they should be complimented for parts of tasks completed and well done, not criticized for the unfinished segment. Finally, in criticizing Menachem's work, Watson was, in effect, directly criticizing Menachem as a person because Mediterranean Judeans do not separate work and personhood as do Americans. This is probably why Menachem reacted so strongly to Watson's statements. He felt that he had to defend himself as a person.

In doing a job, once local persons have done almost all of the job in question, they would feel that others in responsibility should compliment them for that part of the task already completed, not complain about the part that has yet to be done. Witness the many half-completed ancient and modern projects all about the Mediterranean—all worthy of praise, not blame.

Finally, in criticizing a person's work, higher-status persons, in effect, directly criticize the individual as a person because Mediterranean Judeans do not separate work and person as do Americans. Thus because they believe they are defending themselves as persons, Mediterranean Judeans will react quite strongly to any criticism of their performance.

To criticize a person's work is to criticize the person himself or herself. This perspective lurks in the background of the passage in the Gospels where the disciples are criticized, for example, for not fasting (Mark 2:18; Matt. 9:14; Luke 5:33), for picking grain on Sabbath (Mark 2:24; Matt. 12:2; Luke 6:2), for being unable to heal (Mark 9:18; Matt. 17:16; Luke 9:40). All such criticism equally entails a personal criticism of their teacher and his way of living.

This feature is likewise apparent in all the passages in which Paul describes the way his opponents criticize him. Paul does not take criticism well because any criticism of his work calls his very person into doubt! And vice versa: criticism of his moral worth as a person calls his work into doubt. And his opponents do criticize his person, for his enemies say, for example, "His letters are weighty and strong, but his bodily presence is weak, and his speech of no account" (2 Cor. 10:10). Read, from this perspective, his denigration of his opponents in Second Corinthians as "so many, peddlers of God's word" (2:17), or as "false apostles" and in fact servants of Satan (11:13–15), or as "superlative apostles" (12:11). All along, he says, he does not care to defend himself before his Corinthian friends, but only "in the sight of God . . . for your upbuilding, beloved" (12:19).

The same reaction to criticism is found in the letter to the Galatians. There Paul states that he believes the Galatian acceptance of a form of the Christian way of life different from the one he presented is due to the Galatians' being under the spell of the evil eye (Gal. 3:1: "Who has bewitched you?" is literally "Who has cast an evil eye-spell on you?").

There Is Nothing We Don't Know

Howard Stall had been working as an advisor in a farm machinery company in a suburb of Sepphoris. One day he noticed that Jose, a subordinate who had been there for many years, had not been following orders. He had, in fact, been doing things in the way that they had been done before Howard arrived. Howard criticized Jose for not introducing the new methods he had presented to plant employees. Jose became very angry. He told Howard that he knew what he was doing and began to point out things that he felt were wrong with the new system.

Jose's criticisms were really completely irrelevant, yet he shouted at Howard so all in the plant could hear. Howard was somewhat taken aback.

Why did Jose become so angry?

MEANINGS IN WINDOW 45

Challengers to Honor Are to Be Repulsed

Generally speaking, Mediterranean Judeans resent having their work inspected and/or criticized far more than Americans do. In inspecting and criticizing Jose's work, Howard was (unknowingly) belittling Jose's status. Mediterranean Judeans tend to be more sensitive to status differences than Americans, and a denial of status often arouses strong hostility among the Mediterranean Judeans. Such was the case with Jose. The irrelevant criticisms were, of course, an expression of Jose's hostility and an attempt to reduce Howard's status. By yelling them out, Jose was calling the attention of his co-workers (his in-group) to Howard's out-group membership.

Given this perspective, it should be clear that in the Gospel story, those who criticize Jesus, especially in Judea, expect their in-group to rally around them against Jesus, just as Jesus' criticism is to get his in-group in line against his enemies. Window 38 presented the many instances in which Jesus sarcastically asks Torah experts: "Have you not read . . . ?" Such a riposte joins the rejection of a person's role (Torah expert who certainly *has* read) with the person as such. Role and personhood are identified, here as incompetent and/or malicious.

Then consider Jesus' response to the Sadducees' mocking question about levirate (brother-in-law) marriage and the resurrection in Mark 12:18–27:

> And Sadducees came to him, who say that there is no resurrection; and they asked him a question, saying, "Teacher, Moses wrote for us that if a man's brother dies and leaves a wife, but leaves no child, the man must take the wife, and raise up

122

children for his brother. There were seven brothers; the first took a wife, and when he died left no children; and the second took her, and died, leaving no children; and the third likewise; and the seven left no children. Last of all the woman also died. In the resurrection whose wife will she be? For the seven had her as wife."

Jesus said to them, "Is not this why you are wrong, that you know neither the scriptures nor the power of God? For when they rise from the dead, they neither marry nor are given in marriage, but are like angels in heaven. And as for the dead being raised, have you not read in the book of Moses, in the passage about the bush, how God said to him, 'I am the God of Abraham, and the God of Isaac, and the God of Jacob'? He is not God of the dead, but of the living; you are quite wrong."

Notice the direct accusation of their being wrong at the beginning and end of the response. Further they are told quite bluntly that they know neither the scriptures of God nor the power of God. Note, too, that Jesus is speaking to Sadducees, persons who control the Temple and are in charge of the official instruction of the people of Israel. Their work is considered as hopelessly wanting—and so is their personal status, their very persons!

Another approach is to turn the attack around and have the attackers look at their own rather identical behavior: "And if I cast out demons by Beelzebul, by whom do your sons cast them out? Therefore they shall be your judges" (Matt. 12:27; Luke 11:19).

Paul too uses a similar ploy to mark himself off from his opponents; by doing so he expects to get people on his side. In his argument against those urging Christians to be circumcised, Paul pointedly exclaims: "I wish those who unsettle you would mutilate themselves!" (Gal. 5:12). The rather mild "mutilate themselves" means "cut it all off," that is, not just the foreskin. Given the focal symbolism of the male member in Mediterranean society, Paul's exclamation would surely serve to pull in in-group members. He makes similar points in his letter to the Philippians: "Look out for the dogs, look out for the evil-workers, look out for those who mutilate the flesh" (Phil. 3:2), here calling circumcision "mutilation."

These are many instances of criticism of what persons say and do in order to reject them as persons, as out-group.

Honor Before Efficiency

Being the supervisor of a Mediterranean-Judean–American business venture had taught Robert Baran a number of things about how to work with people from another culture. He was musing over some of these things when one of his Mediterranean-Judean subordinates and his American counterpart came in with a joint report they had prepared. Robert took the paper and asked the men to return in about two hours since he would be finished reading the report by then.

When the two men returned, Robert spoke to the Mediterranean-Judean subordinate and told him that he had done a very good job. However, there were some "additions" that should be incorporated. Since the report had to be redone anyway, there were one or two minor changes that he would like to see in the paper.

After the Mediterranean-Judean subordinate left, the American subordinate spoke up. He asked Robert why he had treated the Mediterranean Judean so leniently and not complained about his shoddy work. It was obvious that the Mediterranean Judean had not done his part of the work correctly, and the other man felt that Robert should have reprimanded him. Robert replied that he believed it was best not to be harsh, intimating that perhaps later the other American would understand why.

Why did Robert think it unwise to reprimand the Mediterranean-Judean subordinate?

MEANINGS IN WINDOW 46

Non-hostile Out-Group Persons Are to Be Encouraged

Mediterranean Judeans tend to be oversensitive to criticism (as Americans view it). Mediterranean-Judean workers tend to react to the slightest critical remark as if it were a major threat. The group-oriented ego of the Mediterranean Judean is easily hurt, and he does not take very kindly to criticism. Since Robert had to maintain relationships with the local subordinate, it was quite perceptive of him to praise the subordinate first and then suggest "additions."

In the Gospel tradition, several times Jesus is asked questions that are perceived not to be hostile, so in response he gives the questioner reinforcement and support:

And as he was setting out on his journey, a man ran up and knelt before him, and asked him, "Good Teacher, what must I do to inherit eternal life?" And Jesus said to him, "Why do you call me good? No one is good but God alone. You know the commandments: 'Do not kill, Do not commit adultery, Do not steal, Do not bear false witness, Do not defraud, Honor your father and mother.'" And he said to him, "Teacher, all these I have observed from my youth." And Jesus looking upon him loved him, and said to him, "You lack one thing; go, sell what you have, and give to the poor, and you will have treasure in heaven; and come, follow me." At that saying his countenance fell, and he went away sorrowful; for he had great possessions (Mark 10:17–22).

And one of the scribes came up and heard them disputing with one another, and seeing that he answered them well, asked him, "Which commandment is the first of all?" Jesus answered, "The first is, 'Hear, O Israel: The Lord our God, the Lord is one; and you shall love the Lord your God with all your heart, and with all your soul, and with all your mind, and with all your strength.' The second is this, 'You shall love your neighbor as yourself.' There is no other commandment greater than these." And the scribe said to him, "You are right, Teacher; you have truly said that he is one, and there is no other but he; and to love him with all the heart, and with all the understanding, and with all the strength, and to love one's neighbor as oneself, is much more than all whole burnt offerings and sacrifices." And when Jesus saw that he answered wisely, he said to him, "You are not far from the kingdom of God." And after that no one dared to ask him any question (Mark 12:28–34; Matt. 22:34–40 omits any positive assessment by Jesus).

Note that in both of these passages, the questioner is not described as hostile. Jesus answers in a way befitting an honorable person who may yet wish to maintain relationships with the questioner. Consider the following case where the questioner is described as hostile, yet Jesus takes no note of this. This procedure is highly unusual in the Gospels:

And behold, a lawyer stood up to put him to the test, saying, "Teacher, what shall I do to inherit eternal life?" He said to him, "What is written in the law? How do you read?" And he answered, "You shall love the Lord your God with all your heart, and with all your soul, and with all your strength, and with all your mind; and your neighbor as yourself." And he said to him, "You have answered right; do this, and you will live" (Luke 10:25–28).

Becoming Indispensable

A new American administrator came to Hebron to take over a department of his firm. He thought that it was important that the local Mediterranean-Judean executives be trained so they could teach their skills to others. He was even willing to send a number of the men to the U.S. to receive this training. Upon broaching this idea with one of his subordinates, he was told the following story.

There was a Mediterranean-Judean centurion in Herod's Judean army who was the only one who could order sandals from the supply department because he kept the ordering code under lock and key. He was under constant pressure to fill orders and, in fact, the job was too much for him. One of his subordinates asked "Why not get someone to help you?" The centurion replied, "Are you crazy? As soon as I do that, I would be replaced because I would no longer be needed."

The American administrator was not sure how to take the story and paid little attention to it. A year later he was sorry he had not thought about it more.

Why did the Mediterranean-Judean centurion refuse to recruit someone to help him?

Take Measures to Become Indispensable

Mediterranean-Judean workers tend to view themselves as indispensable, or at least strive to become indispensable. If the Mediterranean-Judean centurion asked for help from a subordinate, the request would be tantamount to an admission that the centurion could be replaced ("as soon as I do that . . . I would no longer be needed"). This, of course, runs counter to the prevalent American cliche that "no one is indispensable."

Now this tendency among Mediterranean-Judean workers to believe themselves indispensable can be found in all walks of life. The reason for this is that the family is the prevailing model of society, and once a child is born into a family, it too is viewed by the in-group as indispensable. Families as a rule cannot imagine their families to be constituted other than with the individuals that now make it up. Parents do not speak of getting rid of this or that child to make up the ideal family. All are led to believe they truly belong in that in-group just because they have been born into that family.

Or, to put it another way, interpersonally intensive societies such as the Mediterranean view organic models and metaphors as most appropriate for explaining situations—all essentially rooted in the organic processes of repro-duction, birth, growth, biological relations, etc. Just as the roles of mother or father, oldest son and youngest son, and gender-based roles in general are given and irrevocable, so, too, are other social roles. There is room in the social fabric for the village idiot and the prophet; both are as indispensable as my mother and my father and my siblings.

Notice how easily Paul's explanation of Christ and the church derives from such an organic model, with each person seen as indispensable:

Now concerning spiritual gifts, brethren, I do not want you to be uninformed. . . .

Now there are varieties of gifts, but the same Spirit; and there are varieties of service, but the same Lord; and there are varieties of working, but it is the same God who inspires them all in every one. To each is given the manifestation of the Spirit for the common good. To one is given through the Spirit the utterance of wisdom, and to another the utterance of knowledge according to the same Spirit, to another faith by the same Spirit, to another gifts of healing by the one Spirit, to another the working of miracles, to another prophecy, to another the ability to distinguish between spirits, to another various kinds of tongues, to another the interpretation of tongues. All these are inspired by one and the same Spirit, who apportions to each one individually as he wills.

For just as the body is one and has many members, and all the members of the body, though many, are one body, so it is with Christ. For by one Spirit we were all baptized into one body—Jews or Greeks, slaves or free—and all were made to drink of one Spirit.

For the body does not consist of one member but of many. If the foot should say, "Because I am not a hand, I do not belong to the body," that would not make it any less a part of the body. And if the ear should say, "Because I am not an eye, I do not belong to the body," that would not make it any less a part of the body. If the whole body were an eye, where would be the hearing? If the whole body were an ear, where would be the sense of smell? But as it is, God arranged the organs in the body, each one of them, as he chose. If all were a single organ, where would the body be? As it is, there are many parts, yet one body. The eye cannot say to the hand, "I have no need of you," nor again the head to the feet, "I have no need of you." On the contrary, the parts of the body which seem to be weaker are indispensable, and those parts of the body which we think less honorable we invest with the greater honor, and our unpresentable parts are treated with greater modesty, which our more presentable parts do not require. But God has so composed the body, giving the greater honor to the inferior part, that there may be no discord in the body, but that the members may have the same care for one another. If one member suffers, all suffer together; if one member is honored, all rejoice together.

Now you are the body of Christ and individually members of it. And God has appointed in the church first apostles, second prophets, third teachers, then work-ers of miracles, then healers, helpers, administrators, speakers in various kinds of tongues. Are all apostles? Are all prophets? Are all teachers? Do all work mira-cles? Do all possess gifts of healing? Do all speak with tongues? Do all interpret? But earnestly desire the higher gifts (1 Cor. 12:1, 4–31).

Here every individual is in fact indispensable in this organic picture of the church. This perception of the indispensability of the individual is likewise rooted in the perception of limited good. One's socially assigned role, the role that one acquires thanks to the help of others and into which one literally "grows" with the help of others, exists as one's piece of the limited social pie. To fall out of or give up the role is to produce a social hole, to the detriment of all in one's network. Dealing with the death of a family member is all about dealing with a hole in the social fabric.

In the modern world, we assume that goods are, in principle, in unlimited supply. If a shortage exists, we can produce more. If one person gets more of something, it does not automatically mean someone else gets less, it may just mean the factory worked overtime and more became available. In this perspective, just as nothing is limited, so too persons can readily be replaced. No one is indispensable. But in the ancient Mediterranean, the perception was quite different. All goods were believed to exist in finite, limited supply. This included not only material goods but social roles, offspring, and qualities such as honor, friendship, love, power, security, and status as well—literally everything in life. The pie could not grow larger; there was only so much to go around, like land in the region. Hence, a larger piece for anyone automatically meant a smaller piece for someone else.

An honorable man would thus be interested only in what was rightfully his and would have no desire to gain anything more, that is, to take what is another's. But each honorable man did in fact have something that was rightfully his. And in the social fabric, what was rightfully his was a social role, indispensably his.

From the viewpoint of occupation and ability, if a Mediterranean Judean asks for help from a subordinate who can in fact take his place, the request would be tantamount to an admission that the one could be replaced by the other and perhaps that the subordinate actually belonged in the role, that the role was usurped.

On the other hand, since status depends on birth, higher-status persons can ask for help from lower-status persons without being thought dispensable, since no lower-status person could ever take the place of a higher-status one. People hiring invite workers to work for them, with no loss of status; but workers must be asked and do not come looking for work (see Matt. 20:1–16, quoted on page 157). Furthermore, every time Jesus is asked a question about Torah-based behavior, an "Is it lawful . . ." question, those asking him are putting him to the test. The reason for this is that if they were serious, they would be recognizing Jesus as an authoritative interpreter of Torah and hence a threat to their indispensable status. So he is always tested:

> And behold, there was a man with a withered hand. And they asked him, "Is it lawful to heal on the sabbath?" so that they might accuse him (Matt. 12:10).

And Pharisees came up to him and tested him by asking, "Is it lawful to divorce one's wife for any cause?" (Matt. 19:3; see Mark 10:2).

Then the Pharisees went and took counsel how to entangle him in his talk. And they sent their disciples to him, along with the Herodians, saying, "Teacher, we know that you are true, and teach the way of God truthfully, and care for no man; for you do not regard the position of men. Tell us, then, what you think. Is it lawful to pay taxes to Caesar, or not?" (Matt. 22:15–17; see Mark 12:13–14; Luke 20:20–22).

Finally, lower-status people can always make requests of higher-status people with no loss of anything. It is this social behavior that lies at the root of praying. People pray to God in the same way that they pray for favors to higher-status persons in their own societies who control their social existence. For example, for most people the most significant higher-status persons in Mediterranean Judea were patrons who did favors for their less-fortunate, lower-status clients in return for honor. In the parable about the householder hiring day laborers (Matt. 20:1–15), a patron would have paid his clients more for their work than a nonpatron. The problem in the parable is that the complainants are paid fairly but not on patron-client terms. Now to call God "Father" is the same as to call him "Patron." To approach God as "Father" is to approach him as "Patron."

A Helping Hand?

Katie Salk was a secretary to one of the administrators of a college in Jerusalem. Because of her position she got to know a number of the Mediterranean-Judean teachers very well.

She found that many of these teachers were extremely overloaded with paper work because of the shortage of clerical help. Therefore, Katie at first tried to help these teachers by offering to do some typing and/or filing for them if they felt they needed it. Their reaction was not what she expected, however. All the teachers refused her offer. And most of them seemed somewhat indignant at the suggestion.

Why did the teachers refuse Katie's offer and appear indignant at her suggestion?

MEANINGS IN WINDOW 48

Do Not Threaten the Indispensability of Others

Katie, by offering to help the teachers, was in effect suggesting that they were incapable of adequately performing their jobs. Hence, they were insulted and refused Katie's offer. Mediterranean Judeans, when accepting a job, will usually not let anyone know that it is too much for them. Such an admission would diminish their personal worth. Thus, it would seem that they are not indispensable, and Mediterranean Judeans place great importance upon being indispensable.

This indispensability is replicated in a number of Mediterranean social traits. As a rule, Mediterranean Judeans, much like other Mediterraneans, fuse their job with their family. A person is considered indispensable both in his or her family position and role and in his or her job position and role. Further, given such indispensability, Mediterraneans generally are unable to conceive of a career change; all careers are forever, like family roles. Traditionally, one's career can serve as one's last name, for example, John the Baptizer, Jesus the Prophet, Paul the Apostle, Joshua the Butcher, etc. Finally Mediterraneans view their residence, their place of living, as stable and unchangeable, just as they believe in the permanence of their neighborhoods.

In the Gospels, note how the fisherman called by Jesus simply follow him. Whether they are capable of doing what Jesus wants is not even at issue (although we may presume they knew what Jesus was after):

And passing along by the Sea of Galilee, he saw Simon and Andrew the brother of Simon casting a net in the sea; for they were fishermen. And Jesus said to them, "Follow me and I will make you become fishers of men." And immediately they left their nets and followed him. And going on a little farther, he saw James the son of Zebedee and John his brother, who were in their boat mending the nets. And immediately he called them; and they left their father Zebedee in the boat with the hired servants, and followed him (Mark 1:16–20; see Matt. 4:18–22).

He went out again beside the sea; and all the crowd gathered about him, and he taught them. And as he passed on, he saw Levi the son of Alphaeus sitting at the tax office, and he said to him, "Follow me." And he rose and followed him (Mark 2:13–14; see Matt. 9:9; Luke 5:27–28).

When the apostles or disciples return from their first preaching-teaching-healing tour, Matthew offers no report, Mark's is muted: "The apostles returned to Jesus, and told him all that they had done and taught" (Mark 6:30), while Luke is quite enthusiastic: "The seventy returned with joy, saying, 'Lord, even the demons are subject to us in your name!'" (Luke 10:17).

Yet incidents reporting that the disciples could not heal in certain instances (e.g., Matt. 17:16; Mark 9:18; Luke 9:40) would indicate that perhaps the picture is painted in too Mediterranean a fashion. For in point of fact, one of those Jesus calls betrays him, another vows to stay with him to the end but abandons him, and all eventually desert him.

Why did Jesus prove such a poor judge of character? In his culture, one does not judge another psychologically, by character, but stereotypically, by expected, external performance. Thus, James and John believe they can do anything involved in discipleship (see Mark 10:35–41, quoted on page 133).

Peter also believes he can do whatever Jesus commands:

Peter said to him, "Even if I must die with you, I will not deny you." And so said all the disciples (Matt. 26:35).

Peter said to him, "Even though they all fall away, I will not" (Mark 14:29).

And he said to him, "Lord, I am ready to go with you to prison and to death" (Luke 22:33).

And ultimately, Paul likewise believes he can do anything required for discipleship. For Paul himself tells us that his call and commission (as prophet/apostle) came directly from God and that he proceeded to do just what God wanted:

But when he who had set me apart before I was born, and had called me through his grace, was pleased to reveal his Son to me, in order that I might preach him among the Gentiles, I did not confer with flesh and blood, nor did I go up to Jerusalem to those who were apostles before me, but I went away into Arabia; and again I returned to Damascus (Gal. 1:15–17).

It was only after fourteen years that he decided to check with those who were with Jesus:

> Then after fourteen years I went up again to Jerusalem with Barnabas, taking Titus along with me. I went up by revelation; and I laid before them (but privately before those who were of repute) the gospel which I preach among the Gentiles, lest somehow I should be running or had run in vain (Gal. 2:1–2).

Becoming Indispensable: Part II

The U.S. Navy often helps in training Judean naval officers and other personnel. It is necessary, therefore, for communications between those two groups to be good. One problem seems to occur over and over again. The American military will have some information in the form of reports, blueprints, etc., which they wish to have distributed to a number of Mediterranean-Judean naval personnel. They will send the information to the proper sources. It often happens, however, that this information will get no farther than the first officer who receives it. Many of the Americans get very upset about this.

Obviously the first Mediterranean-Judean officer kept the information. Why does the first person to get the information keep it from others?

Take Measures to Become Indispensable: Part II

By keeping the information to himself, the first officer to get it increases his control, status, and self-esteem. Keeping the information from the others gives the officer control over it. The officer who keeps the information has access to something that is unavailable to all others in the organization. In other words, the officer increases his power and competitive position within the organization.

Most Mediterranean Judeans are out-group members to other Mediterranean Judeans. This may be true for members of the same organization who compete for promotions. Consider how the sons of Zebedee, family in-group members, can vie for precedence against other members of the Jesus circle, to whom, in this instance, they are out-group:

> And James and John, the sons of Zebedee, came forward to him, and said to him, "Teacher, we want you to do for us whatever we ask of you." And he said to them, "What do you want me to do for you?" And they said to him, "Grant us to sit, one at your right hand and one at your left, in your glory." But Jesus said to them, "You do not know what you are asking. Are you able to drink the cup that I drink, or to be baptized with the baptism with which I am baptized?" And they said to him, "We are able." And Jesus said to them, "The cup that I drink you will drink; and with the baptism with which I am baptized, you will be baptized; but to sit at my right hand or at my left is not mine to grant, but it is for those for whom it has been prepared." And when the ten heard it, they began to be indignant at James and John (Mark 10:35–41).

(Matthew 20:20–28 has the same ending, but has the mother of James and John put the question to Jesus; Luke does not have the incident.)

Persons who get revelations from God, the contents of which they keep to themselves, also have access to something that is unavailable to all others in the organization. In other words, the seer in the know increases his power and competitive position within the organization. This seems to be Paul's position as articulated in Galatians 1:11–24. He does not make known his revelation to anyone but rather eventually begins the task he believes is his (after three years, Gal. 1:18). The same is true of his other revelatory experiences, the contents of which he does not reveal since their concealment is to his benefit within the group:

> I must boast; there is nothing to be gained by it, but I will go on to visions and revelations of the Lord. I know a man in Christ who fourteen years ago was caught up to the third heaven—whether in the body or out of the body I do not know, God knows. And I know that this man was caught up into Paradise—whether in the body or out of the body I do not know, God knows—and he heard things that cannot be told, which man may not utter. On behalf of this man I will boast, but on my own behalf I will not boast, except of my weaknesses (2 Cor. 12:1–5).

This is where secrecy enters. Those who have exclusive access to information kept from others have control over that information and over others upon whom that information bears. In the Gospel tradition, Peter, James, and John were witnesses to Jesus' Transfiguration, which underscored his superiority relative to Moses and Elijah, the Law and the Prophet(s). They were told by Jesus, in Mark and Matthew, not to reveal the event to anyone:

> And as they were coming down the mountain, he charged them to tell no one what they had seen, until the Son of man should have risen from the dead. So they kept the matter to themselves, questioning what the rising from the dead meant (Mark 9:9–10).

> And as they were coming down the mountain, Jesus commanded them, "Tell no one the vision, until the Son of man is raised from the dead" (Matt. 17:9).

Yet in Luke, it seems to be their idea, thus accounting for their privileged position elsewhere in the narrative: "And when the voice had spoken, Jesus was found alone. And they kept silence and told no one in those days anything of what they had seen" (Luke 9:36). Furthermore, note how in Matthew Peter receives numerous revelations (individually or in association with James and John). Controlled access to new information from God is part of his qualification to be leader of the group.

Mind Your Own Opinions

After working in Jerusalem for two months in a Mediterranean-Judean organization, Bill Barton decided to make some suggestions to the Mediterranean Judean who was in charge. He talked about how effective American supervisors had found the brainstorming technique for getting new ideas. Bill explained that a number of people would get together and the problem or topic of discussion would be introduced. Then everyone would give whatever suggestions came to mind and the best ideas would then be utilized.

The Mediterranean-Judean supervisor seemed rather hesitant, but since Bill was supposed to be an expert advisor, the supervisor set up a brainstorming session with his Mediterranean-Judean subordinates in executive positions. All the men got together at 2:00 the next afternoon, and they began with a consideration of the problems facing the company. Then they were all told to reflect upon the problems and to volunteer their opinions concerning the best way to deal with the problems. It became obvious from the long periods of prolonged silence that the process just wouldn't work. No local executive really volunteered anything.

Why did the brainstorming session fail?

MEANINGS IN WINDOW 50

Mistakes and Errors Are Rarely One's Own

Mediterranean Judeans generally do not like to take initiative. Furthermore, initiative and decision making are frequently regarded as unimportant by Mediterranean Judeans. This is because in Judea one is often rewarded or advanced on the basis of making few errors rather than on taking initiative. When working for organizations, Mediterranean Judeans try to avoid making decisions or volunteering directive advice. In this way the chances of an error are reduced, giving the person a greater chance of being rewarded or promoted.

This is replicated in religious language by an emphasis on committing very few sins. Rewards are for avoiding evil, avoiding sin, avoiding occasions of sin—not for doing good, taking initiative for making the good better. The technique for successful living is to maintain one's status and perform for the maintenance of status, not to get ahead. Such status maintenance involves essentially avoiding errors or anything that might be interpreted as an error. Maximum social detachment and a minimum of out-group involvement is the order of the day. Consider Jesus' parable of the Pharisee and the toll collector (often called "publican") in this perspective:

135

He also told this parable to some who trusted in themselves that they were righteous and despised others: "Two men went up into the temple to pray, one a Pharisee and the other a tax collector. The Pharisee stood and prayed thus with himself, 'God, I thank thee that I am not like other men, extortioners, unjust, adulterers, or even like this tax collector. I fast twice a week, I give tithes of all that I get.' But the tax collector, standing far off, would not even lift up his eyes to heaven, but beat his breast, saying, 'God, be merciful to me a sinner!' I tell you, this man went down to his house justified rather than the other; for every one who exalts himself will be humbled, but he who humbles himself will be exalted" (Luke 18:9–14).

In the story, the Pharisee does nothing wrong. He fulfills his obligations to God and, presumably, to his fellow in-group members. The toll collector does not bother listing what he did wrong. The Pharisee's position in the story is conservative: no initiative, just status maintenance, avoiding anything that might be taken as an error or sin. The toll collector's stance indicates one who takes initiative (even to fulfill the position of toll collector requires initiative, traded off perhaps with loss of honor), one who does wrong and perhaps some right. The former person is rather passive, the latter active. This latter type of personality is rare in the culture.

Perhaps this cultural emphasis on avoiding anything wrong (to the detriment of initiative and seeking the betterment of situations instead of simply their restoration to what they were in the past) is replicated in emphasis on one's unknown sins. Leviticus 4 and 5 consider this problem under the following heading: "If anyone sins unwittingly in any of the things which the LORD has commanded not to be done, and does any one of them . . ." (Lev. 4:2). And the psalmist prays, "But who can discern his errors? Clear thou me from hidden faults" (Ps. 19:12).

Know-Who Is What Counts

Drew McAuley ran a factory in first-century Perea. He urgently needed a large electrical device for his firm. When the device arrived at the port of Caesarea, he began the attempt to transport it from the port to the Perean location of his plant. In the process, he had to see some thirty-two officials in order to get the required permissions. Drew spent many hours talking to the "proper" people and getting papers signed. He became very frustrated by all this red tape and even lost his temper a number of times. He was assured by his local friends, however, that the bureaucratic hassle he experienced was quite normal procedure.

Why did Drew have such difficulty in getting permission to move the equipment?

MEANINGS IN WINDOW 51

Responsibility Is to Be Avoided

Mediterranean Judeans are hesitant to accept responsibility. As a result, no one wanted to give Drew permission to move the device he imported. If anyone did, in fact, take responsibility and give permission, he (nowadays, sometimes she) was taking the great risk of being reprimanded by some capricious superior for whatever reasons such a superior might choose to cite. Or the decision might, in fact, be an erroneous one. In Judea, people are promoted more on the basis of how few errors they make than on how effective they are in making decisions. Thus, no one wanted to assume the responsibility of giving Drew the permission he needed. In Mediterranean-Judean society no one in authority cares to give permission for some publicly observable behavior that might be perceived negatively by a superior. Many people in imperial or royal bureaucratic positions fear their judgment will be countermanded by a superior and thus endanger their position in their organization. This was particularly true in the first-century Mediterranean.

This feature of the culture lies behind those devices for group acceptance of responsibility, such as stoning or crowd verdicts. In stoning, no individual actually kills the culprit since all the stones together do. If the group accepts responsibility, no individual has to take any risk in making a judgment, hence no individual in authority is at risk.

Thus, the laws of Leviticus would have people as a group stone those who practice infant sacrifice, practice sorcery, or curse and blaspheme God:

Say to the people of Israel, Any man of the people of Israel, or of the strangers that sojourn in Israel, who gives any of his children to Molech shall be put to death; the people of the land shall stone him with stones (Lev. 20:2).

A man or a woman who is a medium or a wizard shall be put to death; they shall be stoned with stones, their blood shall be upon them (Lev. 20:27).

And the LORD said to Moses, "Bring out of the camp him who cursed; and let all who heard him lay their hands upon his head, and let all the congregation stone him. And say to the people of Israel, Whoever curses his God shall bear his sin. He who blasphemes the name of the LORD shall be put to death; all the congregation shall stone him; the sojourner as well as the native, when he blasphemes the Name, shall be put to death" (Lev. 24:13–16).

The book of Numbers reports a case of required stoning for nonobservance of the Sabbath:

While the people of Israel were in the wilderness, they found a man gathering sticks on the sabbath day. And those who found him gathering sticks brought him to Moses and Aaron, and to all the congregation. They put him in custody, because it had not been made plain what should be done to him. And the LORD said to Moses, "The man shall be put to death; all the congregation shall stone him with stones outside the camp" (Num. 15:32–35).

The book of Deuteronomy requires stoning for a person introducing the worship of other gods; for a recalcitrant son at the parent's request (see Deut. 21:18–21, quoted on page 3); and for certain cases of sexual misconduct (see Deut. 22:13–30).

If your brother, the son of your mother, or your son, or your daughter, or the wife of your bosom, or your friend who is as your own soul, entices you secretly, saying, "Let us go and serve other gods," which neither you nor your fathers have known, some of the gods of the peoples that are round about you, whether near you or far off from you, from the one end of the earth to the other, you shall not yield to him or listen to him, nor shall your eye pity him, nor shall you spare him, nor shall you conceal him; but you shall kill him; your hand shall be first against him to put him to death, and afterwards the hand of all the people. You shall stone him to death with stones, because he sought to draw you away from the LORD your God, who brought you out of the land of Egypt, out of the house of bondage" (Deut. 13:6–10).

If there is found among you, within any of your towns which the LORD your God gives you, a man or woman who does what is evil in the sight of the LORD your God, in transgressing his covenant, and has gone and served other gods and worshiped them, or the sun or the moon or any of the host of heaven, which I have forbidden, and it is told you and you hear of it; then you shall inquire diligently, and if it is true and certain that such an abominable thing has been done in Israel, then you shall bring forth to your gates that man or woman who has done this evil thing, and you shall stone that man or woman to death with stones (Deut. 17:2–5).

The book of Joshua has a case of a clan head and his group, Achan of the tribe of Judah, defrauding God by absconding with some things "devoted to God," that is booty that was to be destroyed in the conquest of the inhabitants of the land. Because Achan had disobeyed God,

> Joshua and all Israel with him took Achan the son of Zerah, and the silver and the mantle and the bar of gold, and his sons and daughters, and his oxen and asses and sheep, and his tent, and all that he had; and they brought them up to the Valley of Achor [literally, "trouble"]. And Joshua said, "Why did you bring trouble on us? The LORD brings trouble on you today." And all Israel stoned him with stones; they burned them with fire, and stoned them with stones. And they raised over him a great heap of stones that remains to this day; then the LORD turned from his burning anger. Therefore to this day the name of that place is called the Valley of Achor (Josh. 7:24–26).

In the parable of the householder and his vineyard, we read that "the tenants took his servants and beat one, killed another, and stoned another" (Matt. 21:35). And in Jesus' plaint against Jerusalem: "O Jerusalem, Jerusalem, killing the prophets and stoning those who are sent to you! How often would I have gathered your children together as a hen gathers her brood under her wings, and you would not!" (Matt. 23:37; Luke 13:34).

John has Jesus frequently on the verge of being stoned by Judean opponents, clearly for blasphemy:

> Jesus answered, "If I glorify myself, my glory is nothing; it is my Father who glorifies me, of whom you say that he is your God. But you have not known him; I know him. If I said, I do not know him, I should be a liar like you; but I do know him and I keep his word. Your father Abraham rejoiced that he was to see my day; he saw it and was glad." The [Judeans] then said to him, "You are not yet fifty years old, and have you seen Abraham?" Jesus said to them, "Truly, truly, I say to you, before Abraham was, I am." So they took up stones to throw at him; but Jesus hid himself, and went out of the temple (John 8:54–59).

> "I and the Father are one."
> The [Judeans] took up stones again to stone him. Jesus answered them, "I have shown you many good works from the Father; for which of these do you stone me?" The [Judeans] answered him, "It is not for a good work that we stone you but for blasphemy; because you, being a man, make yourself God." Jesus answered them, "Is it not written in your law, 'I said, you are gods'? If he called them gods to whom the word of God came (and scripture cannot be broken), do you say of him whom the Father consecrated and sent into the world, 'You are blaspheming,' because I said, 'I am the Son of God'? If I am not doing the works of my Father, then do not believe me; but if I do them, even though you do not believe me, believe the works, that you may know and understand that the Father is in me and I am in the Father" (John 10:30–38).

> Then after this he said to the disciples, "Let us go into Judea again." The disciples said to him, "Rabbi, the [Judeans] were but now seeking to stone you, and are you

going there again?" Jesus answered, "Are there not twelve hours in the day? If any one walks in the day, he does not stumble, because he sees the light of this world. But if any one walks in the night, he stumbles, because the light is not in him" (John 11:7–10).

In Luke, the Jerusalem authorities who challenge Jesus fear the city residents: "But if we say, 'From men,' all the people will stone us; for they are convinced that John was a prophet" (Luke 20:6). A similar fear of the people protects Peter and John in Acts: "And some one came and told them, 'The men whom you put in prison are standing in the temple and teaching the people.' Then the captain with the officers went and brought them, but without violence, for they were afraid of being stoned by the people" (Acts 5:25–26). Likewise in Acts, there are a number of stoning incidents, beginning with Stephen (7:58), then some of the brethren (14:5), and Paul (14:19). As for crowd verdicts, surely the most famous is that of the Judean residents of Jerusalem in the account of Jesus' condemnation and death (see Matt. 27:15–26, quoted on page 115).

Note how whole groups or crowds speak at one time in the Gospels. Of course this never happens in real life. Yet by ascribing a statement to a group or a crowd, the authors witness to the perspective that no individual actually makes a decision to express a given idea but rather that the whole group does. The following sampling is from Matthew although other New Testament narratives reveal the same procedure. And every speaking group forms an in-group in the narrative episode.

And they went and woke him, saying, "Save, Lord; we are perishing" (Matt. 8:25).

And the men marveled, saying, "What sort of man is this, that even winds and sea obey him?" (Matt. 8:27).

Then the disciples of John came to him, saying, "Why do we and the Pharisees fast, but your disciples do not fast?" (Matt. 9:14).

Then he left the crowds and went into the house. And his disciples came to him, saying, "Explain to us the parable of the weeds of the field" (Matt. 13:36).

But when the disciples saw him walking on the sea, they were terrified, saying, "It is a ghost!" And they cried out for fear (Matt. 14:26).

And those in the boat worshiped him, saying, "Truly you are the Son of God" (Matt. 14:33).

Then the disciples came and said to him, "Do you know that the Pharisees were offended when they heard this saying?" (Matt. 15:12).

And they discussed it among themselves, saying, "We brought no bread" (Matt. 16:7).

At that time the disciples came to Jesus, saying, "Who is the greatest in the kingdom of heaven?" (Matt. 18:1).

When the disciples heard this they were greatly astonished, saying, "Who then can be saved?" (Matt. 19:25).

And when he entered Jerusalem, all the city was stirred, saying, "Who is this?" (Matt. 21:10).

When the disciples saw it they marveled, saying, "How did the fig tree wither at once?" (Matt. 21:20).

And they sent their [the Sadducees'] disciples to him, along with the Herodians, saying, "Teacher, we know that you are true, and teach the way of God truthfully, and care for no man; for you do not regard the position of men" (Matt. 22:16).

As he sat on the Mount of Olives, the disciples came to him privately, saying, "Tell us, when will this be, and what will be the sign of your coming and of the close of the age?" (Matt. 24:3).

Afterward the other maidens came also, saying, "Lord, lord, open to us" (Matt. 25:11).

But when the disciples saw it, they were indignant, saying, "Why this waste?" (Matt. 26:8).

Now on the first day of Unleavened Bread the disciples came to Jesus, saying, "Where will you have us prepare for you to eat the passover?" (Matt. 26:17).

And plaiting a crown of thorns they put it on his head, and put a reed in his right hand. And kneeling before him they mocked him, saying, "Hail, King of the [Judeans]!" (Matt. 27:29).

So also the chief priests, with the scribes and elders, mocked him, saying: "He saved others; he cannot save himself. He is the King of Israel; let him come down now from the cross, and we will believe in him. He trusts in God; let God deliver him now, if he desires him; for he said, 'I am the Son of God'" (Matt. 27:41–43).

Mind Your Own Status

Simeon ben Raphael was a Mediterranean-Judean physician who had received some of his training and experience in the United States and was an expert in internal medicine. When he returned to Judea, he was placed under the supervision of an older physician who had been at the hospital for many years. After his second day on the job, he met an American physician who was visiting the hospital, and they made the rounds of the hospital together. During their rounds, the American noticed that the younger Mediterranean-Judean physician read a prescription given by the older physician that the younger man knew to be quite erroneous, even harmful to the patient. Yet he did not change the orders that had been given by the older man. The American thought this was unethical.

How can the behavior of Simeon ben Raphael be explained?

MEANINGS IN WINDOW 52

Superiors Are Always Right

Mediterranean Judeans consider it very shameful behavior to contradict a superior. Better that others suffer and die rather than a person shame himself or herself by contradicting a superior. Then, too, consider the shame the superior would have to undergo should he (or she) be proven wrong. And furthermore, as previously indicated, Mediterranean Judeans are not expected to take the initiative or make suggestions. This, again, arises from the fact that they are rewarded for not making errors. Thus, by avoiding decisions, the chances of making an error are reduced and the chances of promotion are increased.

With this principle in mind, consider the following parable:

As they heard these things, he proceeded to tell a parable, because he was near to Jerusalem, and because they supposed that the kingdom of God was to appear immediately. He said therefore, "A nobleman went into a far country to receive a kingdom and then return. Calling ten of his servants, he gave them ten pounds, and said to them, 'Trade with these till I come.' But his citizens hated him and sent an embassy after him, saying, 'We do not want this man to reign over us.' When he returned, having received the kingdom, he commanded these servants, to whom he had given the money, to be called to him, that he might know what they had gained by trading. The first came before him, saying, 'Lord, your pound has made ten pounds more.' And he said to him, 'Well done, good servant! Because you have been faithful in a very little, you shall have authority over ten cities.' And the second came, saying, 'Lord, your pound has made five pounds.'

And he said to him, 'And you are to be over five cities.' Then another came, saying, 'Lord, here is your pound, which I kept laid away in a napkin; for I was afraid of you, because you are a severe man; you take up what you did not lay down, and reap what you did not sow.' He said to him, 'I will condemn you out of your own mouth, you wicked servant! You knew that I was a severe man, taking up what I did not lay down and reaping what I did not sow? Why then did you not put my money into the bank, and at my coming I should have collected it with interest?' And he said to those who stood by, 'Take the pound from him, and give it to him who has the ten pounds.' (And they said to him, 'Lord, he has ten pounds!') 'I tell you, that to every one who has will more be given; but from him who has not, even what he has will be taken away. But as for these enemies of mine, who did not want me to reign over them, bring them here and slay them before me'" (Luke 19:11–27).

Note first of all that the king is quite severe and generally vicious. He plunders others, gloats over his enemies, and takes pleasure at having those enemies killed in his presence. Obviously the first two servants were like the king, profiting by taking advantage of others, hence equally vicious. For this they are rewarded. The proper behavior in the culture is that of the third servant, who is quite faithful in the task of maintaining things the way they were before the king left and not taking any initiative, not taking any risks. For this he is punished!

This is one of several parables of Jesus in which the scenario presents a slice of life lived by reprobate or immoral persons. It is not unlike the proverb, "The day of the Lord will come like a thief in the night" (1 Thess. 5:2). It would take us too far afield at this point to explain the point of such parables. However, it ought to be clear that God or the Lord is not to be identified with the thief; nor is the behavior of the thief offered as an example to be followed. It is the suddenness, randomness, and unexpected nature of a thief's coming into one's house that is underscored in the proverb.

Back to Mediterranean culture, older colleagues with power of recommendation are to be complied with. This principle is a replication of a cultural value that ranks persons on the same social level in terms of birth rank. In society at large, older persons are to be respected, and within a kinship group, first-born children within their own gender claims come first. For example, Laban wishes his daughters to marry according to birth rank: "Laban said, 'It is not so done in our country, to give the younger before the first-born'" (Gen. 29:26). Similarly, firstborn sons outrank all others:

And they sat before him [Joseph], the first-born according to his birthright and the youngest according to his youth; and the men looked at one another in amazement (Gen. 43:33).

The precedence of the firstborn figures prominently in the Exodus story, as is well known. It likewise figures prominently in the theological assessment of Jesus as Messiah:

For those whom he foreknew he also predestined to be conformed to the image of his Son, in order that he might be the first-born among many brethren (Rom. 8:29).

He is the image of the invisible God, the first-born of all creation (Col. 1:15).

He is the head of the body, the church; he is the beginning, the first-born from the dead, that in everything he might be preeminent (Col. 1:18).

. . . and from Jesus Christ the faithful witness, the first-born of the dead, and the ruler of kings on earth. To him who loves us and has freed us from our sins by his blood . . . (Rev. 1:5).

As for respecting older persons the tone is set by Leviticus 19:32: "You shall rise up before the hoary head, and honor the face of an old man, and you shall fear your God: I am the LORD." The social value of older persons is that they remember the past and serve as living references:

> Hear this, you aged men,
>   give ear, all inhabitants of the land!
> Has such a thing happened in your days,
>   or in the days of your fathers?
> Tell your children of it,
>   and let your children tell their children,
>   and their children another generation (Joel 1:2–3).

Early Christian leaders were to be equally respectful toward older Christians: "Do not rebuke an older man but exhort him as you would a father; treat younger men like brothers, older women like mothers, younger women like sisters, in all purity" (1 Tim. 5:1–2). On the other hand, older persons lost their credibility by arguing with younger persons. Honor demanded that they simply not take younger persons that seriously:

> Do not be ashamed to instruct the stupid or foolish
>   or the aged man who quarrels with the young.
> Then you will be truly instructed,
>   and will be approved before all men (Sir. 42:8).

Sirach's basic advice is:

> Do not disregard the discourse of the aged,
>   for they themselves learned from their fathers;
> because from them you will gain understanding
>   and learn how to give an answer in time of need (Sir. 8:9).
>
> You have gathered nothing in your youth;
>   how then can you find anything in your old age?
> What an attractive thing is judgment in gray-haired men,
>   and for the aged to possess good counsel!

How attractive is wisdom in the aged,
    and understanding and counsel in honorable men!
Rich experience is the crown of the aged,
    and their boast is the fear of the Lord (Sir. 25:3–6).

Thus for a younger professional or bureaucrat to correct or contradict a higher-level, older fellow professional or bureaucrat would be to endanger chances for promotion, whether in the military or the bureaucracies of the period.

More on Making Friends

Pat and Mike were U.S. army officers stationed in a camp outside Jerusalem. Both men were required to do a lot of work with the local Mediterranean-Judean soldiers, both in joint projects and in certain types of training. Mike noticed that Pat learned a little Aramaic and asked the Mediterranean Judeans how they were, what was happening, and the like. He also noticed that occasionally Pat would give the Mediterranean Judeans a cigarette or do some other small favor for them.

Mike, on the other hand, maintained his rank and composure at all costs, feeling that if he did not do so he would lose the respect of his men. As it turned out, however, the teams with which Pat worked always seemed to do as well or better than Mike's. Mike also noticed that Pat was having a lot more fun than he was because Pat was constantly getting invitations to go to the beach or out to dinner. All of this confused Mike.

Why did Pat's groups usually do better than Mike's?

MEANINGS IN WINDOW 53

All Non–Out-Group Relations Are Personal Relations

By showing interest in the Mediterranean-Judean soldiers and learning some of their language and customs, Pat was behaving as Mediterranean Judeans expect a leader to behave. Thus, they were willing to work for him. The supervisor-subordinate relationship in Judea is much more personal than in the United States. By showing concern for the Mediterranean-Judean soldiers, Pat came to be regarded both as a good leader and as a friend. That is, the soldiers thought of him as a member of their in-group. This also explains why he also received many social invitations. It is important to realize that the leader should remain somewhat aloof in order to maintain status. It is expected, however, that he show concern and interest in his workers. Apparently, Pat was able to show concern and maintain status at the same time. This illustrates the Mediterranean belief that all non–out-group relationships are personal relationships.

In this context, consider the requirements for Christian supervisors (bishops) and managers (deacons). These requirements in Timothy parallel those required of a Roman general, whose task it was to serve as mentor for well-born, elite youth fulfilling their military rung on a career ladder (*cursus honorum*).

146

The saying is sure: If any one aspires to the office of bishop, he desires a noble task. Now a bishop must be above reproach, the husband of one wife, temperate, sensible, dignified, hospitable, an apt teacher, no drunkard, not violent but gentle, not quarrelsome, and no lover of money. He must manage his own household well, keeping his children submissive and respectful in every way; for if a man does not know how to manage his own household, how can he care for God's church? He must not be a recent convert, or he may be puffed up with conceit and fall into the condemnation of the devil; moreover he must be well thought of by outsiders, or he may fall into reproach and the snare of the devil.

Deacons likewise must be serious, not double-tongued, not addicted to much wine, not greedy for gain; they must hold the mystery of the faith with a clear conscience. And let them also be tested first; then if they prove themselves blameless let them serve as deacons. The women likewise must be serious, no slanderers, but temperate, faithful in all things. Let deacons be the husband of one wife, and let them manage their children and their households well; for those who serve well as deacons gain a good standing for themselves and also great confidence in the faith which is in Christ Jesus (1 Tim. 3:1–13).

For a bishop, as God's steward, must be blameless; he must not be arrogant or quick-tempered or a drunkard or violent or greedy for gain, but hospitable, a lover of goodness, master of himself, upright, holy, and self-controlled; he must hold firm to the sure word as taught, so that he may be able to give instruction in sound doctrine and also to confute those who contradict it. For there are many insubordinate men, empty talkers and deceivers, especially the circumcision party; they must be silenced, since they are upsetting whole families by teaching for base gain what they have no right to teach (Titus 1:7–11).

In the ancient Mediterranean world, the tendency of analysts like Paul or the author of the post-Pauline letters was to look at social arrangements in the Roman Empire in terms of the kinship group. So relations to superiors in the Empire will not be very different from relations of family members to the father.

Let every person be subject to the governing authorities. For there is no authority except from God, and those that exist have been instituted by God. . . . Therefore one must be subject, not only to avoid God's wrath but also for the sake of conscience (Rom. 13:1, 5).

Be subject for the Lord's sake to every human institution, whether it be to the emperor as supreme, or to governors as sent by him to punish those who do wrong and to praise those who do right (1 Peter 2:13–14).

However, in the Christian community, people in charge of the group did not actually have any legal standing as did officials of the Empire. Their authority was not like that of a father in the family, who did, indeed, have legal power. However, since kinship relationships did serve as model for understanding roles in Christian groups, it would seem that the main male role in the family in which a person was in charge but had no rights was that of the mother's brother (Latin, *avunculus*; German, *Oheim*; Medieval English, *Em*). It was the role and status of the mother's brother that served for Christian leadership in their fictive kin group of "brothers" and "sisters":

> Now, brethren, you know that the household of Stephanas were the first converts in Achaia, and they have devoted themselves to the service of the saints; I urge you to be subject to such men and to every fellow worker and laborer (1 Cor. 16:15–16).

> Likewise you that are younger be subject to the elders. Clothe yourselves, all of you, with humility toward one another, for "God opposes the proud, but gives grace to the humble" (1 Peter 5:5).

But in the family, an extended family that might include married sons as well as slaves:

> Wives, be subject to your husbands, as is fitting in the Lord. Husbands, love your wives, and do not be harsh with them. Children, obey your parents in everything, for this pleases the Lord. Fathers, do not provoke your children, lest they become discouraged. Slaves, obey in everything those who are your earthly masters, not with eyeservice, as men-pleasers, but in singleness of heart, fearing the Lord. Whatever your task, work heartily, as serving the Lord and not men, knowing that from the Lord you will receive the inheritance as your reward; you are serving the Lord Christ (Col. 3:18–24; see also Eph. 5:22–6:9).

We might note that in early Christian writings, the word "obey" is directed only to children and slaves, who are to obey their fathers (and mothers) and masters (and mistresses). On the other hand, the word is applied to all human beings relative to God: all are to "obey" God.

Small Is Beautiful, of Course

Norm Scholenby was working on a Ph.D. in business administration. He felt that a good project would be to investigate certain cross-cultural differences in organizational structure. To this end, he decided to compare some of the big American organizations with Mediterranean-Judean organizations. The results of his initiative got him a trip to Judea to examine these organizations first-hand. After a very brief exposure to a few organizations, Norm was struck by two obvious differences:

1. There were really no "big" industries in the Mediterranean by American standards.

2. There was no concept of "middle management" in Mediterranean-Judean companies—there was just the boss and the employees.

It took Norm another month or so before he began to understand the cultural reasons for these differences.

What were the cultural reasons for these differences?

MEANINGS IN WINDOW 54

Economics and Religion Are Embedded in Kinship and Politics

Family businesses have long been a tradition in Judea, as elsewhere in the Mediterranean (and aside from foreign multinationals, this ideal has not changed much in recent times). The perception of society in terms of in-group and out-group as well as the intense in-group–out-group competition in Judea tend to make large firms unmanageable. Family businesses have dominated the Mediterranean economy largely because such businesses can be operated solely by in-group members (the family, by definition, being the primary in-group). Furthermore, Mediterranean-Judean employers tend to be very reluctant to put nonfamily members in trusted positions such as "middle management." As a result, middle management was virtually nonexistent in ancient Judea, perhaps apart from Roman governmental enterprises where such managers were often slaves.

As a rule, Mediterranean businesses have been embedded in families or in governments, ranging from city-state to kingdom to empire. In other words, traditionally, the Mediterranean has evidenced both domestic economy and political economy, but no "economy" as a distinctly perceived, free-standing social institution. This means that aside from governmental enterprises (e.g., today, railways, oil import and export, refineries, food imports, radio and television, schools, etc.), there are really no large privately owned industries. As a matter of fact, one might say that as a rule wherever privately owned "big" industries begin on the north shore of the Mediterranean, there the Mediterranean world ends.

The Romans succeeded in organizing the Mediterranean in terms of large power structures, never in terms of large economic structures. The main generalized symbolic medium of social interaction was power sanctioned by force, never wealth sanctioned by goods and service. Roman religion, like Israelite religion, was embedded in politics as well as in kinship. There was political religion and domestic religion. Political religion was the official religion of the state, with official state support and worship for the benefit of the whole population and its head(s). Domestic religion looked to the domestic group and its concerns, largely fertility in humans, animals, and fields, as well as concern for ancestors.

If Jesus had religious concerns in the Gospel story, it is obvious that they looked to political religion, the revitalization of the house of Israel. This was the overall in-group, with the rest of humankind of little concern. Consider such old traditions as Jesus' directive: "Go nowhere among the Gentiles, and enter no town of the Samaritans, but go rather to the lost sheep of the house of Israel" (Matt. 10:5–6). Or consider Jesus' words to the Greek woman in the region of Tyre and Sidon: "Let the children first be fed, for it is not right to take the children's bread and throw it to the dogs" (Mark 7:27). Matthew's tradition prefaces that remark with Jesus saying "I was sent only to the lost sheep of the house of Israel. . . . It is not fair to take the children's bread and throw it to the dogs" (Matt. 15:24, 26).

Keep It in the Family

Beni ben Beni and Harv Swan were buddies when they were employed by the Judean army's corps of engineers. Harv, an American stationed in Judea with the U.S. army, was assigned to work with Beni, an officer with the Judean army. Subsequently both of them worked together on a number of construction projects. In that way they got to know each other very well. They decided that when they were discharged, they would set up a small construction business together.

Six months later, when both men were out of the service, they got together to plan the establishment of their business. Everything went well until they started discussing hiring practices. Beni said, "Well, my brother can supervise this division. I have a cousin who can be in charge of this other group, and a number of other friends will want to take positions as well." Harv told Beni that he thought they should interview people and choose those people who they believed were best qualified. A heated argument ensued, and the two men finally decided to drop the whole thing.

How would you account for the failure of the joint enterprise?

MEANINGS IN WINDOW 55

In Everything the Family Comes First

The differences between Mediterranean-Judean and American standards for operating a business were simply too great. In most Mediterranean-Judean businesses, one places only in-group members in positions of trust. A good businessman will rely almost entirely on his family (slaves, children, brothers, cousins, and friends). Hence, Beni wanted to rely almost entirely on his brother, cousin, and friends. In an American business, these positions are filled (at least ideally) by those who are most competent. While Americans are willing to give preference to their competent friends, the concept of an in-group, based on belonging and not on competence, is virtually alien to most American businesses. Hence relatives and friends of the employer are hired only infrequently (often even when the relatives and/or friends are competent). Given these cultural differences, it is not surprising that the joint enterprise was abandoned.

Notice that all "economic" institutions referred to in the Gospels are run by households (including a master and slaves, father and sons, father, mother, sons, persons hired for a time, wives and children, and the like) or by governments (king and slaves or subjects, centurion, Roman procurator).

151

However, one must likewise note that the differences between Mediterranean-Judean and American standards are equally great in other social institutions. U.S. and Mediterranean standards have little in common when it comes to the assessment of being religious and moral, or norms for the proper running of government, or standards for family living and parenting. In every case, in-group is primary in the Mediterranean. In-group is defined or delimited in terms of family rules. In-groups thus work in terms of fictive kinship bonds and boundaries. Status rankings, too, derive from family rules, with gender and age precedence recognized in all areas of life, and overall social standing determined by a family's inherited social ranking or "honor."

These observations about economics are significant because they relate rather directly to religion. The fact is that before the Industrial Revolution of the nineteenth century, all business was in the hands of either a family or a government. Economy was either domestic economy or political economy. And the same was true of religion until the Enlightenment. There was both domestic religion and political religion, but no religion pure and simple. What this means is that for Jesus to deal with the religion of his day in a public way was to deal with political religion. On the other hand, when Christianity spread outside of Judea, it formed groupings of "brothers and sisters," hence domestic religion of a sort. It is largely from such a domestic religious arrangement that we have our New Testament documents.

Before the time of Emperor Constantine (early fourth century A.D.), the Christian church was run like a local family. Its sanctions were those of a family, rooted in commitment activation or a sense of honor and belonging. Deviants were dishonored, ostracized, shunned. It was religion embedded in a fictive kin group consisting of brothers and sisters in Christ. In its economic aspects such as care for travelers, the poor, widows, and orphans, it was run like a family business, that is, a domestic economy.

But after the emperor Constantine, the Christian church became embedded in the government with sanctions of power rather than family commitment and belonging. The church's sanctions became those of government, rooted in power. Deviants were banished, beaten, killed. Church officials became government officials, with the emperor representing Christ. It now was religion embedded in politics, a theocracy. Its economic aspects such as salaries for clergy, care for the poor, widows, and orphans were run as governmental concerns, that is, a political economy. Nongovernmental economic enterprises remained embedded in family. Households often maintained their traditional domestic religion with its concerns for fertility and ancestors. On the other hand, the old church form of religion embedded in kinship—domestic religion—emerged in monasticism.

SUMMARY WINDOW

The Mediterranean-Judean work setting served as the focus for the preceding episodes. We learned that job security often depends on avoiding mistakes. Workers are frequently promoted on this basis (making few mistakes) rather than on job performance. One result is that Mediterranean-Judean workers are reluctant to take initiative, because beginning something new increases the chances of error. Also, Mediterranean-Judean workers tend to be very sensitive to criticism, partly because they feel so insecure about their jobs and partly because their honor is always at stake. If criticisms of the workers are to be made, they must be made with discretion. Finally, we noted that Mediterranean-Judean employers tend to place only family or in-group members in positions of trust.

FOR FURTHER READING

Elliott, John H. "Patronage and Clientism in Early Christian Society: A Short Reading Guide." *Forum* 3/1 (1987): 39–48.

Malina, Bruce J. "Dealing with Biblical (Mediterranean) Characters: A Guide for U.S. Consumers." *Biblical Theology Bulletin* 19 (1989): 127–141.

Oakman, Douglas E. "Was Jesus a Peasant? Implications for Reading the Samaritan Story (Luke 10:30–35)." *Biblical Theology Bulletin* 22 (1992): 117–125.

Rohrbaugh, Richard L. "The Pre-Industrial City in Luke-Acts: Urban Social Relations." In *The Social World of Luke-Acts: Models for Interpretation*, edited by Jerome H. Neyrey. Peabody, Mass.: Hendrickson, 1991, 125–151.

VIII

CONCEPT OF
TIME

INTRODUCTORY WINDOW

The ancient Mediterranean cultural preference when it came to time was the present. Mediterraneans, like peasants the world over, were essentially present-oriented. Future orientation is possible only in societies in which all one's basic present needs, such as food, clothing, and shelter, are taken care of. In societies where the acquisition and preparation of necessities takes most of each day, people are present-oriented.

Furthermore, this present covered a rather broad swath of the process of living. It is very unlike industrial watch time, where the click of the second hand marks a fleeting present. This broad present consisted of all that had occurred within one's remembrance as well as all that was forthcoming because already at hand in some way. The birth of a pregnant wife's child, the crop of a growing field, the festival marked by an emerging moon were all present, since they were forthcoming (and not future, as we might think).

Significant events always began when significant persons arrived for those events—and so they always began on time. Ancient Mediterraneans differed quite radically from modern Americans when it came to time.

Clock Time and Event Time

George Smith, in his retirement, took his U.S. savings and bought himself a rather large vineyard in the Eastern Mediterranean, specifically in first-century Galilee. He moved into the house on the place along with his wife. He could not ask his own married children to come since they had their own lives to live. The vines were growing well, but now it was time to trim back the vines and hoe around the plants. George needed help since he could not possibly do the work himself. So he went to the village square and put up a sign announcing work at his place beginning August 8 at 9 A.M. He figured a number of the men he always saw hanging around the village square would see the sign and show up for work. He would offer them several weeks' work, and they would be happy with the income and the security over the next month or so.

The entire first week after the sign went up passed, with no one showing up at his place. The same happened the next week. George got angry and decided he would have to do the work himself.

How would you account for the apparent indifference of the Mediterranean Judeans that George wished to hire?

New Testament Persons Are Concerned About the Present

Mediterranean Judeans did not share the same abstract concept of time that Americans have. There were really no clocks or watches available to first-century people. "Hour" of day might be announced in cities by means of a change of guard, but in villages a rough estimate of the time of day was based on a combination of individual internal time (when one was hungry, tired, etc.) and location of the sun. Similarly, there were no calendars available to most people. The day (not date) would be known only by information on the phase of the moon determined by Temple officials and duly announced. Times were remembered in terms of significant events (for example, "the year the war with Rome began"). And significant events were recorded in terms of significant people holding public office (for example, dating Jesus' birth by Caesar Augustus and Quirinius, the governor of Syria, in Luke 2:1–2). Similarly, "on time" occurs when significant persons come on the scene (see Window 57).

Mediterranean Judeans were essentially present-oriented. Without clocks or calendar, there was little interest in the abstract future. To be on time meant to arrive upon being summoned and before some significant personage or to arrive on some agreed-upon day, determined by moon or feast.

Now consider the behavior of a first-century Mediterranean householder, born and raised in the culture:

> For the kingdom of heaven is like a householder who went out early in the morning to hire laborers for his vineyard. After agreeing with the laborers for a denarius a day, he sent them into his vineyard. And going out about the third hour he saw others standing idle in the market place; and to them he said, "You go into the vineyard too, and whatever is right I will give you." So they went. Going out again about the sixth hour and the ninth hour, he did the same. And about the eleventh hour he went out and found others standing; and he said to them, "Why do you stand here idle all day?" They said to him, "Because no one has hired us." He said to them, "You go into the vineyard too." And when evening came, the owner of the vineyard said to his steward, "Call the laborers and pay them their wages, beginning with the last, up to the first." And when those hired about the eleventh hour came, each of them received a denarius. Now when the first came, they thought they would receive more; but each of them also received a denarius. And on receiving it they grumbled at the householder, saying, "These last worked only one hour, and you have made them equal to us who have borne the burden of the day and the scorching heat." But he replied to one of them, "Friend, I am doing you no wrong; did you not agree with me for a denarius? Take what belongs to you, and go; I choose to give to this last as I give to you. Am I not allowed to do what I choose with what belongs to me? Or do you begrudge my generosity?" So the last will be first, and the first last (Matt. 20:1–16).

Consider the work relations and hiring practices in this Mediterranean-Judean private business. The householder expected to have a number of laborers available to him at the time he needed them. He recruits them personally throughout the day: presumably at the first, third, sixth, ninth, and eleventh hours. He recruits in the same place, it seems, always finding new people at that location to hire. He does not become impatient with any of them, even though he might have used all hands from the morning on. That same day he pays the workers for their work, giving each person the same wage, regardless of the hours put in. When some get irritated at this, he accuses them of having the evil eye (v. 15: "Is your eye evil because I am good?"). What sort of businessman is this?

Being on Time

Henry Rogers and his wife had been in first-century Palestine for about four weeks and were having a wonderful time. Henry was a visiting military attache at Pilate's Antonia Fortress and had met a number of Mediterranean Judeans during his first few weeks there. Henry and his wife decided to have a dinner party for all their new Mediterranean-Judean friends. They asked about what time the Mediterranean Judeans ate in the evening, and they were told it was shortly after sundown. The invitations were made for everyone to come shortly after sundown for cocktails and dinner. Mrs. Rogers figured everyone could have a drink or two and that dinner would be served somewhat after sundown when all had arrived.

However, a good while after sundown, only half of the guests had arrived and the dinner was getting cold. By the late-night watch when everyone had arrived, both Henry and his wife were very upset and angry and the atmosphere was very strained.

How would you account for the tardiness of the Mediterranean-Judean guests?

MEANINGS IN WINDOW 57

In the New Testament, Significant Persons Always Come on Time

Mediterranean Judeans did not emphasize promptness nearly so much as Americans if only because there was no measure by which to gauge promptness. They had no watches or calendars, only sun location, cock crowing, moon phases, and the like. The custom was to invite people, then send someone to inform them that everything was ready (see Matt. 22:2–3). For a Mediterranean Judean a social invitation for "shortly after sundown" meant anytime after sundown and before normal bedtime, rather than exactly a very short time after sundown.

However, not all Mediterranean Judeans used "Mediterranean-Judean time" in all circumstances. Many working with Roman officials in the country and some Jerusalemite urban Judeans used Roman military criteria, specifically the announcement of watches of the day. As a result half of those invited arrived promptly shortly after sundown and the other half some two hours later (by U.S. reckoning). One must be prepared for this much variety when dealing with promptness.

Consider the time determination in the following passages from the New Testament:

> Then the kingdom of heaven shall be compared to ten maidens who took their lamps and went to meet the bridegroom. Five of them were foolish, and five were wise. For when the foolish took their lamps, they took no oil with them; but the wise took flasks of oil with their lamps. As the bridegroom was delayed, they all slumbered and slept. But at midnight there was a cry, "Behold, the bridegroom! Come out to meet him." Then all those maidens rose and trimmed their lamps. And the foolish said to the wise, "Give us some of your oil, for our lamps are going out." But the wise replied, "Perhaps there will not be enough for us and for you; go rather to the dealers and buy for yourselves." And while they went to buy, the bridegroom came, and those who were ready went in with him to the marriage feast; and the door was shut. Afterward the other maidens came also, saying, "Lord, lord, open to us." But he replied, "Truly, I say to you, I do not know you." Watch therefore, for you know neither the day nor the hour (Matt. 25:1–13).

The tarrying of the bridegroom is typical; central personages in a social event need not pay attention to time limits. When he arrives, he is always "on time." The bridegroom's unconcern for those expected to be awake to meet him is likewise typical of the central personage in a social event. Those others are to be sure to be ready when the bridegroom comes. The time the bridegroom comes is on time; after that everyone else is "late." The doors may now be closed.

> Now he told a parable to those who were invited, when he marked how they chose the places of honor, saying to them, "When you are invited by any one to a marriage feast, do not sit down in a place of honor, lest a more eminent man than you be invited by him; and he who invited you both will come and say to you, 'Give place to this man,' and then you will begin with shame to take the lowest place. But when you are invited, go and sit in the lowest place, so that when your host comes he may say to you, 'Friend, go up higher'; then you will be honored in the presence of all who sit at table with you. For every one who exalts himself will be humbled, and he who humbles himself will be exalted" (Luke 14:7–11).

In this story, the presupposition is that the eminent man arrives after others have, requiring room to be made for him. A further presupposition is that the eminent man is always on time. Finally, an elegant meal would require the host to summon those invited when everything was ready:

> The kingdom of heaven may be compared to a king who gave a marriage feast for his son, and sent his servants to call those who were invited to the marriage feast (Matt. 22:2–3).

Mediterranean Time Is Different

When he first arrived in first-century Palestine, Louis Lance spent a lot of time with his brother Les, who had been there for many years. One afternoon while the brothers were sitting in Les's office discussing some work they were doing, one of Les's Mediterranean-Judean subordinates stopped by to leave a report he had completed. Les remembered that they were having a party that weekend and invited the Mediterranean Judean to his home when sabbath ended, at sundown. The latter politely replied "Yes, I'd love to. Is that Mediterranean time or American time?" Les laughed and said "Mediterranean time." Louis was not sure what this was all about.

What is meant by the phrase "Mediterranean time"?

In the New Testament, Whenever Events Occur, They Are on Time

By U.S. standards, the Mediterranean-Judean attitude toward time is far more "casual." First-century Mediterraneans had no way to determine precise clock time or precise calendar time. Americans tend to place a premium on being "punctual." For them the hands on the clock mark the present, everything else being past or future. Mediterranean Judeans do not focus on the "punctual." Their present time is a broad period marked by the presence of distinguished persons or significant events in some process. The point is that in this context, Mediterranean time means "sometime after Sabbath, at sundown." American time means "approximately 9:00 P.M."

Consider the following biblical passages:

> Take heed, watch; for you do not know when the time will come. It is like a man going on a journey, when he leaves home and puts his servants in charge, each with his work, and commands the doorkeeper to be on the watch. Watch therefore—for you do not know when the master of the house will come, in the evening, or at midnight, or at cockcrow, or in the morning—lest he come suddenly and find you asleep. And what I say to you I say to all: Watch (Mark 13:33–37).

Here the accurate parts of the day are listed as the evening, at midnight, cockcrow, and the morning. To add to the confusion, Judean and Greek custom saw the new day beginning at sundown, while Romans had the new day beginning at midnight. Once again (and in all the "watch" parables), the exact time is when the important personage arrives, as with the man on the journey in this parable. When he comes is exactly when servants should be ready to receive him in his home.

Now consider Luke's version:

> Let your loins be girded and your lamps burning, and be like men who are waiting for their master to come home from the marriage feast, so that they may open to him at once when he comes and knocks. Blessed are those servants whom the master finds awake when he comes; truly, I say to you, he will gird himself and have them sit at table, and he will come and serve them. If he comes in the second watch, or in the third, and finds them so, blessed are those servants! (Luke 12:35–38)

Luke designates the time of night with the Roman watch hours used in cities, thus "second watch, . . . third watch." The main point, again, is that punctuality occurs when the significant personage arrives, not when some impersonal gauge determines it.

Time Without Clocks

The American military and the Roman military work together on a number of projects in first-century Palestine. There are generally good relations between the two groups. On occasion, however, certain misunderstandings occur. For example, every year some of the Americans attend the graduation of the Judean military trainees for the Roman army. This past year the Americans were not sure when the ceremony was to be held. They got their invitations for the ceremony on the Friday before the Sunday on which it was to take place. Needless to say, many of the Americans were very upset because they had to rearrange their plans. Clearly the Roman-Judean military personnel sent the invitations out quite late ("late," that is, in terms of American standards).

How would you account for the apparent tardiness on the part of the Roman Judeans?

MEANINGS IN WINDOW 59

New Testament Persons See the Forthcoming
Rooted in the Present

Roman-Judean conceptions of time and planning tend to differ drastically from those held by Americans. The Mediterranean people in general have had difficulty in planning successfully for millennia because the future orientation that such planning requires can exist only in a society where all present needs are fully taken care of. Mediterranean people have never enjoyed such a situation until relatively recent times. Theirs have been subsistence economies, never economies of abundance. Furthermore, their plans have typically been foiled by brigandage, wars, and uprisings against central powers, which further made the present uncertain. One result is that much Mediterranean-Judean work behavior appears unsystematic. Little attention to detail and little evidence of careful planning are characteristics of Mediterranean-Judean behavior. Furthermore, estimates of time are likely to be inaccurate and there is little concern with the actual time it takes to complete a task. Nevertheless, much work gets done by means of sheer enthusiasm and devotion to duty.

To take note of Mediterranean present-orientation, consider the proverbs cited by Jesus, which focus solely on the present time: "Therefore do not be anxious about tomorrow, for tomorrow will be anxious for itself. Let the day's own trouble be sufficient for the day" (Matt. 6:34). Likewise notice how Jesus

162

expected to be given power by God in the present, during the lifetimes of people about him: "Truly, I say to you, there are some standing here who will not taste death before they see that the kingdom of God has come with power" (Mark 9:1; Matt. 16:28; Luke 9:27).

Mediterranean Judeans do not feel that it is very important to strictly adhere to schedules as do Americans. For most Mediterraneans, it is the present that counts, while for most Americans, it is the future that counts. The Mediterranean is a present-oriented society, but people do look to the past when the present breaks down, and they wish to find an explanation. Since human nature is always the same, one can look to the past to explain the present. People almost never look to the future for a solution to present ills.

The first feature, that is, the non-importance of schedules, can be observed in the fact that despite all of the statements of the Gospel tradition claiming messianic power for Jesus "before this generation passes away," such manifestations of power simply never happened. The attitude of those for whom it did not happen is seen in the Emmaus disciples (see Luke 24:15–21, quoted on page 167). Further New Testament explanations of what in fact did happen are as follows: Jesus' being raised by God proves beyond doubt that he is the Messiah, but he has not yet come as Messiah with power, as effective Messiah. For example, in one of Peter's speeches in Acts, we read:

> Repent therefore, and turn again, that your sins may be blotted out, that times of refreshing may come from the presence of the Lord, and that he may send the Christ appointed for you, Jesus, whom heaven must receive until the time for establishing all that God spoke by the mouth of his holy prophets from of old (Acts 3:19–21).

Then Paul cites an early Christian hymn at the beginning of Romans, when he speaks of "the gospel concerning God's Son,"

> who was descended from David according to the flesh and designated Son of God in power according to the Spirit of holiness by his resurrection from the dead, Jesus Christ our Lord (Rom. 1:3–4).

Obviously, Jesus' exercise of power as Messiah was forthcoming (not future). The Gospel tradition noted as much:

> And he said to them, "Truly, I say to you, there are some standing here who will not taste death before they see that the kingdom of God has come with power" (Mark 9:1).

Matthew and Luke are slightly different, but all make the same point: the kingdom with power is forthcoming, before "this generation" passes:

> Truly, I say to you, there are some standing here who will not taste death before they see the Son of man coming in his kingdom (Matt. 16:28).

> But I tell you truly, there are some standing here who will not taste death before they see the kingdom of God (Luke 9:27).

In this tradition, then, to "see that the kingdom of God has come with power," to "see the Son of man coming in his kingdom," and to "see the kingdom of God" are quite synonymous. The point here is, according to the tradition, that Jesus expected some of his contemporaries to witness the event. Yet the event did not occur. This sort of outcome would not discourage a Mediterranean with an outlook of "nothing ventured, nothing gained." Even the seer of Revelation believed those responsible for Jesus' death would see him soon with power:

> Behold, he is coming with the clouds, and every eye will see him, every one who pierced him; and all tribes of the earth will wail on account of him. Even so. Amen (Rev. 1:7).

Traditionally, only God knows the future. Once the coming of Jesus as Messiah with power was judged no longer forthcoming, it was left up to God and ceased to be a matter of daily present-oriented concern:

> But of that day or that hour no one knows, not even the angels in heaven, nor the Son, but only the Father (Mark 13:32).

> But of that day and hour no one knows, not even the angels of heaven, nor the Son, but the Father only (Matt. 24:36).

> So when they had come together, they asked him, "Lord, will you at this time restore the kingdom to Israel?" He said to them, "It is not for you to know times or seasons which the Father has fixed by his own authority" (Acts 1:6–7).

Furthermore, when the present breaks down and apparently offers little hope for crisis resolution, people can look into the scriptures (the past) to discern what is forthcoming in the present. This is not looking to the future. It is looking to the past to find out what is happening now.

What nineteenth-century European theologians called "eschatology" and "apocalyptic" are not about a delayed coming of Jesus or disappointment in the early church. Rather, those passages dealing with the "end of the age" consist of citations from the past, the scriptures of Israel, intended to shed light on the present. It is the present that is the focus of interest in such Bible passages. This is true even when biblical authors look into the scriptures of the past in order to shed light on what is forthcoming at present, what is already underway at present.

Focus on the present and its continued impact is evidenced among those who follow Jesus on the basis of the part of his career that has in fact been completed, that is, Jesus as prophet and healer. Others underscored the forthcoming, that is the "unfinished segment" of Jesus' career, his role of "Messiah with power." Jesus' forthcoming role as the one appointed by God to be Messiah with power should not be allowed to conceal his career as prophet and healer. For present-oriented persons, the time when that forthcoming part of Jesus' career gets under way does not really matter much. As a matter of fact, it may even be future!

This is the perspective found in the Gospels. These documents were formulated in Christian groups that no longer believed Jesus' coming with power to be forthcoming. It was something future, known only to God, and left to God. What of our present? Jesus is reported to have cited two proverbs really typical of the present orientation of the culture: "Therefore do not be anxious about tomorrow, for tomorrow will be anxious for itself. Let the day's own trouble be sufficient for the day" (Matt. 6:34). In this present orientation, the Gospels offer guidance for those followers of Jesus on the basis of his career thus far. Matthew offers a system of directives in the Sermon on the Mount and rules for the Christian community. Mark explains how present discipleship entails suffering and how such suffering can lead to triumph. Luke explains the origins of the Christian movement in Jesus and its spread from Jerusalem through agents such as Peter and especially Paul.

Even the writings of Paul change their orientation. While 1 Thessalonians sees Jesus' coming as mighty Lord in power, described in terms of an imperial visit or "parousia" (1 Thessalonians 5), as forthcoming, with 1 Corinthians and subsequent writings this hope dissipates in favor of concern with present Christian group behavior. For Paul it was that part of Jesus' career most recently completed that counted, that is, Jesus' being raised from the dead after an ignominious death, and the implications of this resurrection.

In any event, both for the Gospel communities as for Paul, it was on the basis of that part of Jesus' career already accomplished, not on what yet had to be done, that persons were to follow Jesus.

Scheduling for the Present

Tom Brown wanted to have a lantern installed in the courtyard in front of his house. He went to see a local craftsman. The Mediterranean Judean craftsman promised that he would come the next afternoon. When the craftsman failed to show up, Tom stopped by again and was assured that the lantern would be installed the next day. This happened four times before the craftsman finally came. Of course, Tom was furious because he had been forced to stay in to wait for the craftsman. The "crowning blow" occurred when the craftsman finally arrived. He said that he had forgotten something and then failed to return. Tom decided to do without the lantern.

How would you account for the inability of the craftsman to complete the task on time?

All Plans in the New Testament Are Tentative

We have already noted that until relatively recent times, the Mediterranean-Judean cultural environment, like the Mediterranean culture in general, was harsh enough to make successful planning virtually impossible. One result is that most of the people remained present-oriented. When faced with a problem not solvable by immediately present solutions, people would look to the past. The way heroes of the past faced difficulties or the directives of God's word in scripture from the past would provide present guidance in default of other indications. Now such preference for the present, with a back-up preference for the past, has an interesting result. And that result is that estimates by Mediterranean Judeans of the time required for the future completion of any job, any task, any plan, are likely to be inaccurate. This was the case with the craftsman.

The significant point here is that Mediterranean estimates of the time required to complete any job are likely to be extremely inaccurate, as are Mediterranean estimates of any dimension of the future. This is the case with Jesus' estimate of when God would intervene with power on behalf of God's people. At least this point is clearly evidenced in the Gospels. Similarly this feature applies to early Christian estimates of when Jesus would begin functioning as Messiah with power. In both cases, the answer was a present-oriented "soon" (and not some future calculations).

Consider Luke's account of the disciples on the way to Emmaus:

166

That very day two of them were going to a village named Emmaus, about seven miles from Jerusalem, and talking with each other about all these things that had happened. While they were talking and discussing together, Jesus himself drew near and went with them. But their eyes were kept from recognizing him. And he said to them, "What is this conversation which you are holding with each other as you walk?" And they stood still, looking sad. Then one of them, named Cleopas, answered him, "Are you the only visitor to Jerusalem who does not know the things that have happened there in these days?" And he said to them, "What things?" And they said to him, "Concerning Jesus of Nazareth, who was a prophet mighty in deed and word before God and all the people, and how our chief priests and rulers delivered him up to be condemned to death, and crucified him. But we had hoped that he was the one to redeem Israel. Yes, and besides all this, it is now the third day since this happened" (Luke 24:15–21).

Note the present orientation of the disciples. Their hope "that he was the one to redeem Israel" is typical of their peasant "nothing ventured, nothing gained" attitude. Their hopes were not shattered, just set aside for another person. By the way, the introductory phrase, "Are you the only visitor to Jerusalem . . ." directed by Cleopas to Jesus, is a typical peasant put-down to a fellow group member who should be in the know with the rest of the group. The put-down immediately puts the one answering the question in control and verbally into the space of the questioner.

In this vein, consider the estimates of early Christians in the following passage:

And now, brethren, I know that you acted in ignorance, as did also your rulers. But what God foretold by the mouth of all the prophets, that his Christ should suffer, he thus fulfilled. Repent therefore, and turn again, that your sins may be blotted out, that times of refreshing may come from the presence of the Lord, and that he may send the Christ appointed for you, Jesus, whom heaven must receive until the time for establishing all that God spoke by the mouth of his holy prophets from of old (Acts 3:17–21).

In these words attributed to Peter, we find that Jesus is the Christ or Messiah appointed "for you" (that is, for Israel). His coming as Messiah is delayed "until the time for establishing all that God spoke by the mouth of his holy prophets from of old." Hence one must look to the past, the prophets, to find out when God would now, in the present period, send Jesus as Messiah with power.

Present Orientation

A couple of young American businessmen were interested in starting their own company in first-century Palestine. They asked a number of Mediterranean Judeans whether it would be possible to obtain widespread financial support from local Mediterranean-Judean merchants. Their friends told them that the chances were quite bad and that obtaining Mediterranean-Judean financial backing would be extremely difficult.

After pursuing the matter further the Americans discovered that many Mediterranean Judeans did not even really use money like Americans do. Rather they bought land as soon as feasible, and with income in the form of crops, produce, and livestock, bought precious metals such as gold and silver, often in the form of high-value coins generally not in use, and kept these hidden at home. Investment capital, loans, and credit were simply unavailable on an impersonal business basis. The Americans thought this was rather strange.

How would you account for the reluctance of the Mediterranean Judeans to invest in the enterprise?

MEANINGS IN WINDOW 61

The Only Sensible Investment Is in the Present

Investment, of course, requires a certain amount of planning ahead. The Mediterranean-Judean people would have been hard pressed to plan for the future and in fact were quite skeptical of any such future-oriented ventures.

Consider the physical and social environment in the region. It was an environment subject to sudden, sweeping changes due to climate (drought, earthquake) as well as to social behavior: invasions and war for political profit, slavery to pay debts, insurrection to gain honor through power, brigandage to challenge and shame opponents, taxation rates, and the like. Given available communication techniques, people were uncertain as to when force would be used to pillage and plunder or when a new ruler and a new taxation system would befall them. Consequently, attempts to plan ahead would have generally been futile.

Furthermore, the only "investment" that was believed to yield steady returns was land. And land was the prime target of Romans and various colonists who sought land and its steady production to maintain their honorable positions in the various cities in which they lived. The Mediterranean economy suffered from great fluctuation in the value and availability of coinage. Barter and payment in kind were the norm. Conversion of goods into coinage with later conversion of the coinage into goods was practiced at times, for example, in paying tithes and certain taxes. For elite Mediterranean Judeans, land was the only way to ensure that social fluctuations did not wipe out the value of one's usually inherited wealth. Wealth that could not be turned into land was then hoarded in the form of precious metals, usually gold and silver, at home.

Note that even for a project that might take several years, it was necessary to have all eventualities covered in the present rather than hope for anything in the future. This is a present-oriented mentality, as we see in the following:

> For which of you, desiring to build a tower, does not first sit down and count the cost, whether he has enough to complete it? Otherwise, when he has laid a foundation, and is not able to finish, all who see it begin to mock him, saying, "This man began to build, and was not able to finish" (Luke 14:28–30).

In this description, the construction is viewed as a single, present process even if it takes several years. Costs for the total construction must be in hand, so that one has enough to finish were it all done in the present. Clearly, if one is expected to have all costs covered for a long-term project, the culture does not allow for money-credit, time-payments, and the like. These are the result of future-orientation. Not finishing is shameful, provoking mocking on the part of others.

This same time orientation can be noted in the following parable about going to war. Even though a process such as war takes place over a period in the future, it is considered a single event rooted in present planning. Present planning embraces the forthcoming:

> Or what king, going to encounter another king in war, will not sit down first and take counsel whether he is able with ten thousand to meet him who comes against him with twenty thousand? And if not, while the other is yet a great way off, he sends an embassy and asks terms of peace (Luke 14:31–32).

SUMMARY WINDOW

The Mediterranean-Judean conception of time, like the Mediterranean conception of time in general, is present oriented. In terms of value-orientation preferences, the category time includes the following preferences: first the present, second the past, and should all else fail, then the future. Mediterraneans, then, deal with present anomalies by looking to the past: the word of God in scripture, recourse to history, a consideration of genealogy and ancestors. Americans, on the other hand, choose the future first, the present second, and the past last. When dealing with difficulties in realizing future plans, Americans look to the present: to psychology and the social sciences to explain the present with a view to predicting and making the future realizable, livable, more certain.

Because for Mediterraneans, the present is a broad sweep often embracing a whole process, promptness is not so important in first-century Palestine. American promptness derives really from focus on the future that cuts the actual present extremely short (one second, one minute, now). Further, for Mediterraneans planning for the future does not play a very significant role in the culture if only because all such plans must be already realized in some way in the present. The present realization and control of the future leaves little room for true future planning, with options, creative adaptation, risk, and the like. None of these were present in Mediterranean society as cultural options.

FOR FURTHER READING

Malina, Bruce J. "Christ and Time: Swiss or Mediterranean." *Catholic Biblical Quarterly* 51 (1989): 1–31.

Lauer, Robert H. *Temporal Man: The Meaning and Uses of Social Time.* New York: Praeger, 1981.

Pilch, John J. *Hear the Word, Vol. 2: Introducing the Cultural Context of the New Testament.* Mahwah, N.J.: Paulist Press, 1991.

CONCLUDING
OVERVIEW

The preceding Windows on the world of Jesus look into the following areas:

I. Honor and Shame. The culture is rooted in honor and shame as pivotal values. Honor refers to an individual or collective claim to worth along with the social acknowledgment of that worth. To have shame is to be concerned about one's honor; to be shamed is to lose honor.

1. The status of a father on the social ladder entails his being obeyed and treated respectfully by his children, especially in public. To procrastinate with a command or to disobey is to dishonor.
2. A father symbolizes the family's honor to the outside. All females are embedded in some male, whose task it is to defend the honor of females as well as their own and that of the group.
3. An attack on one's honor requires a forceful defense, a response that will put the attackers on the defensive. Such a successful defense of honor in the social "game" of challenge and response results in renewed grants of honor.
4. Adultery is part of the honor challenges and responses. Adultery means challenging the honor of a male by having sexual relations with the females embedded in him, that is, his family members: wife, unmarried daughter, guests.
5. To express gratitude to an equal means to call a halt to ongoing social interaction. "Thank you" to a social equal, more or less, means "No more, thank you." Expression of gratitude, in certain circumstances, can be a challenge to honor.
6. It is the obligation of upstanding persons to defend the honor of persons who are extremely prominent on the social scale. This would include God, the king and his family, the high priest and his family, local aristocrats who serve as patrons, and the like.
7. A teacher gains honor by winning and keeping the assent and loyalty of a following; this following indicates to the community that the teacher in question is in fact a teacher, hence worthy of honor.

II. General Interpersonal Behavior. Again, it is an interpersonally intensive society. Success in a difficult situation derives from a network of friends. There are no reliable governmental, political services.

8. Personal boundaries are drawn quite differently than in the U.S. The boundaries are looser, embracing more persons in the sense of self.
9. The open expression of emotions is highly valued, especially among males.
10. Certain expressions (such as crying) reflect specific emotional states, much in the way that certain behaviors reflect specific positions within a status hierarchy. The Mediterranean is noted for specific behavior patterns with specific emotions. Reactions to emotional states are quite specific. Thus behaviors and corresponding emotional states can be turned on and off accordingly.
11. Character and performance are essentially intertwined, and a person must be judged by both in a task situation.
12. People in task situations are assessed by more than performance. They are judged, for example, by intention, emotional states, social status, character, etc.
13. Little value is placed on another's being alone or alone with another person. In-group persons are free to wander in and out or stay.
14. Age is a status determiner.
15. A certain amount of formality must exist between superiors and subordinates.
16. Lower-status persons will test superiors to see what they can get away with (authority is disdained, unless it is in-group authority).
17. Bargaining for a fair price is normal—to find a fair price according to one's status.

III. In-Group. Groups are clearly marked off from each other by a set of imaginary lines, so to speak. Those within the lines form the in-group. In-group members are to be supported at all times and at all costs. In-group members merit friendly treatment and favors; out-group persons are to be treated with indifference, even hostility.

18. Mediterraneans will attempt to help friends whenever possible, given the nature of circumstances.
19. People who live next to each other on more or less good terms are in-group members. It is their duty to help one another without remuneration.
20. People living in the same apartment building, village section, or city section see each other as members of the same in-group and feel free to behave accordingly.
21. People from the same village (or city section) when found on alien territory are in-group members. Hence they will be of help to each other if possible.

22. Landlord-tenant relations are preferably in-group relations, with mutual help expected.
23. Employers who show concern for employees and their families are usually placed in the employees' in-group and win their support and devotedness.
24. In-group boundaries constantly shift, depending on the social space where a person is.
25. One helps one's in-group members first. The family marks the center of the in-group.
26. In-laws are in-group members, and one helps in-group members whenever and wherever possible.
27. Longstanding acquaintances are in-group members. In-group members are expected to put themselves out for one another.

IV. Intra-family Relations. The family is the focal institution in the system, with family norms serving as the main analogue for relations in other institutions.

28. People view the world in terms of gender, with males superior simply because they are males.
29. There is a clear gender division of labor, with females in the house and for the house, and males outside the house.
30. Parents talk largely of their children's accomplishments because they reflect the parents' own worth (in-group). They are not much concerned about their value to society (or to the church).
31. Mothers are in charge of children in youth. They see to the well-being and school application of sons. Again the mother-son bond is considered extremely close. Sons are a mother's best insurance in old age.
32. Achievements of sons reflect upon the merits of the mother.

V. Out-Group. The out-group, like the in-group, can have shifting boundaries. However just as the kinship group is the primary in-group, so all other ethnic groups form the primary out-group. Thus Judeans distinguished themselves from all other ethnics ("Gentiles"). However when the political horizon grew prominent after Alexander the Great, persons who considered themselves civilized in the ancient Mediterranean ("Greeks") set themselves off from all others, called "Barbarians."

33. People in face-to-face contact who do not show concern for each other are presumed to be out-group members.
34. Strangers always belong to out-groups since only face-to-face groups where a person can express concern for others can become in-groups.
35. In-group requests for favors can be denied only with good reason, duly explained.

36. Favors by in-group members must be shown proper appreciation.
37. A refusal to perform an in-group request leaves a person in the out-group.
38. Sarcastic joking is a tool of attack, proper to out-group members.

VI. Loving-Kindness (Debt of Gratitude). People who are bound to one another by in-group ties feel obligated to be of assistance to fellow in-group members. This obligation is a sort of "debt of gratitude."

39. Loyalty to one's in-group is required by "loving-kindness" (love, mercy). To be successful in business one must break with one's in-group, hence break off one's in-group ties and obligations. Successful business people are without honor.
40. The fulfillment of distasteful obligations to one's in-group is required by loving-kindness (love).
41. Loving-kindness demands that one always side with a member of the in-group during an argument, whether he is correct or not. Loving-kindness demands that one be a good host.

VII. Common Values. Mediterraneans have as their chief task to maintain the status that they inherited by birth. Status maintenance, as prime concern, is replicated in unwillingness to take risks, take the initiative, admit ignorance, or make errors.

42. One is generally rewarded (promoted) on the basis of seniority, loyalty to the organization, and lack of mistakes during one's career.
43. It is shameful to admit ignorance of or inability to perform functions relating to one's job.
44. It is not necessary to adhere to schedules very strictly. One deserves praise for a job half done rather than blame for a job half undone. To criticize a person's job performance is to criticize the person him/herself since job and person cannot be separated.
45. To criticize one's work is to belittle one's status.
46. Because Mediterranean Judeans are raised with a grandiose sense of self, the slightest critical remark is a major threat.
47. Honor demands one consider him/herself indispensable. One should take measures to become, in fact, indispensable.
48. When accepting a job, honor demands that one not admit inability or ignorance of phases of the job.
49. Secrecy and deception in the work group to maintain indispensability and therefore honor, are quite acceptable, especially toward out-group fellow workers.
50. Since one is promoted for not making mistakes, initiative and decision making are frequently regarded as unimportant.

51. People are not rewarded for effective decision making or for taking responsibility but for not making errors.
52. To avoid errors, one should avoid decision making and criticizing older colleagues, even when they are patently wrong.
53. Supervisors are to show interest in and concern for their subordinates as well as maintain their status and thus win in-group status.
54. Larger businesses are essentially all family businesses with family members alone allowed as "middle managers" (due to out-group hostility).
55. Positions of trust and responsibility in a business go only to family members. Competence is not a major concern.

VIII. Conception of Time. The culture is interpersonally intensive. So what would be considered "on time" is the presence of some person, including the self, when I arrive. Functional, technological explanations are secondary.

56. Mediterranean time, like peasant time in general, is marked by a present orientation with this present covering a broad period.
57. The prompt time to begin is when the significant or central person arrives.
58. On time or punctual is the present seen as a broad period marked by the presence of distinguished persons or significant events in some process.
59. Mediterranean-Judean society is marked by the inability for successful planning of the future (since present needs are never really taken care of).
60. Estimates of time required to do anything are inaccurate (since future orientation is lacking).
61. People in the ancient Mediterranean are quite skeptical about future-oriented ventures, such as investments, if only because of their primary preference for the present.